CONTEMPORARY ENGLISH
BOOK 4

Elizabeth Minicz

Kathryn Powell

CB

CONTEMPORARY BOOKS

a division of NTC/CONTEMPORARY PUBLISHING GROUP
Lincolnwood, Illinois USA

Liz wants to thank Robert Maganini and James Brandman—two terrific doctors—who gave her the gift of life.

Kathryn would like to thank Liz Minicz for inviting her on the project and for her creative drive, friendship, and sense of humor despite all odds. Kathryn also thanks her entire family for their support (direct or via phone and email) and all her students, whose lives inspired many of the scenes depicted in the book.

Both authors would like to thank Roseanne Mendoza for creating an atmosphere of creative deference to us as writers; she has a wonderful way of making perceptive comments while at the same time trusting that we ultimately know where the piece is going and can best hone it.

Cover Illustration: Regan Dunnick

Story on page 117 adapted from "The Mountain God and the River God" from *Stories We Brought With Us,* 1/e by Carol Kasser and Ann Silverman, © 1994. Reprinted by permission of Prentice-Hall, Inc., Upper Saddle River, NJ.

ISBN: 0-8092-0710-9

Contents

Scope and Sequence: Literacy

Unit	Topic	Culture Focus	Literacy Skills	Functions	SCANS Competencies
Unit A	Preliteracy		Shape recognition, directionality, recognizing, tracing, copying uppercase letters		Foundation Skills
Unit B	Preliteracy		Shape recognition, directionality, recognizing, tracing, and copying lowercase letters; matching uppercase and lowercase letters; numbers 1–10		Foundation Skills
1	Human Relations: Greetings	Greetings at school and work	Interpreting and identifying ideographs signifying male and female; sight word recognition	Greetings; stating one's name	Foundation Skills
2	Numbers	Counting	Recognizing, tracing, and copying numbers; matching numbers and quantities; understanding numbers 1–20	Repeating words for clarification	Foundation Skills
3	Home and Neighborhood: Home	Filling out forms	Understanding simple street addresses; identifying name, city, and address on a simple form; matching words and pictures; copying and writing phone numbers and addresses	Identifying; requesting information	Foundation Skills
4	Transportation and Travel: Directions	Getting to know your town	Understanding simple directions and spatial orientation; sight word recognition; matching numbers and quantities; identifying room numbers and sequence on a simple diagram; understanding numbers 21–30	Identifying; asking for clarification; requesting information	Foundation Skills
5	People and Machines: Time	U.S. attitudes toward time	Understanding time and reading clocks; reading signs with business hours indicated; reading analog clocks; understanding numbers 31–60	Showing gratitude; telling time	Foundation Skills
6	Home and Neighborhood: Family	Sharing family information	Understanding words for family members; identifying family members and talking about family; reading simple biographical information forms; copying personal information onto a simple form; numbers in the tens, from 10 to 100	Identifying; demonstrating	Foundation Skills
7	Employment and Opportunity: Jobs	Mini-résumés	Understanding job titles; identifying job titles, times, and phone numbers in simple job ads; sight word recognition; reading the year in figures; recognition of work signs	Expressing state of being	Foundation Skills
8	Consumer Economics: Money	Shopping	Reading prices and price tags; reading symbols for dollars and cents; identifying amounts on coins and paper money; relating prices to coins and bills; adding and subtracting amounts of money	Requesting information; expressing gratitude	Foundation Skills
9	Healthy Living: Food	Groceries	Identifying food items; reading names of food items; reading labels and ads for food; writing prices	Requesting information; giving information	Foundation Skills

Scope and Sequence: Book I

Unit	Topics	Culture Focus	Functions	Grammar	SCANS Competencies
Introductory	Numbers; alphabet	Missing people	Greetings; taking leave; asking for information	Simple commands	Foundation Skills: listening, speaking, reading, writing
1	Human Relations: occupations; place of origin; filling out forms; giving personal information	Family and relatives; a family tree	Asking for information; introductions; giving personal information	*Be*: present affirmative and negative statements and contractions; subject pronouns; *be + from*	Work with cultural diversity; interpret and communicate information
2	Employment and Opportunity: applying for a job; jobs and activities	Supervisors and levels of organization; organization charts	Expressing needs; asking for information, giving answers; making offers	Present of *be*, yes/no questions, short answers; singular and plural nouns; *this* and *that*	Understand systems; organize and maintain information
3	Community Services: school and community; drugs in schools; U.S. drug, alcohol, and nicotine use	Volunteer and community workers	Telling about people; expressing wants	Possessive adjectives; prepositions of place; affirmative and negative commands	Teach others; allocate human resources
4	Home and Neighborhood: neighbors; helping people; child care and babysitters; child care coops	Neighbors helping each other	Refusals; telling about activities; asking for clarification	Present continuous statements and yes/no questions, short answers	Allocate time; negotiate
5	Healthy Living: healthy food; the food pyramid; fast food; planning healthy food	Fast food in the United States	Expressing likes and dislikes; ordering; expressing disagreement; expressing needs	Simple present, affirmative and negative; yes/no questions and short answers	Improve and design systems; participate as a member of a team
6	Transportation and Travel: travel by car, road signs, colors of cars; car maintenance	The importance of cars in the United States	Expressing likes and dislikes; apologizing; asking for information	Wh-questions with *be*; introductory *It*; information questions with simple present	Allocate money; interpret and communicate information
7	Consumer Economics: paying bills; job experience and office skills; wages, salaries, and raises	Minimum wage in the United States	Asking for suggestions; making suggestions; talking about ability and inability	*Can*, affirmative, yes/no questions and short answers; prepositions of time	Allocate human resources; exercise leadership
8	Arts and Entertainment: sports; cable and network television; amount of TV people watch per week	Cable and network television	Giving information and asking for information about the past; speculating about the past; expressing dissatisfaction	*Be*, past, affirmative and negative statements, yes/no questions and short answers	Acquire and evaluate information
9	History and Geography: famous women in U.S. history; Susan B. Anthony; voting	Mary Lyon, who founded Mt. Holyoke	Complimenting; talking about past activities	Simple past (statements, yes/no questions, short answers, information questions)	Organize and maintain information; understand systems
10	People and Machines: phones and phone cards; ATM cards; international calls	Smart cards with computer chips	Talking about plans; expressing necessity; making suggestions; talking about possibility	Future with *going to*: statements, yes/no questions, short answers, information questions; compound sentences	Monitor and correct performance; teach others

Scope and Sequence: Book 2

Unit	Topics	Culture Focus	Functions	Grammar	SCANS Competencies
1	Human Relations: school, company-sponsored training; elementary school, adult education	Asking for clarification on the job	Asking for and giving information; asking for and giving directions; introductions	Present of *be* in affirmative / negative statements, questions; past of *be*; possessives	Work with diversity; sociability, understand organizational systems
2	Arts and Entertainment: relaxation and leisure; going to the zoo; activity schedule, being busy, stress on the job	Stress on the job	Comparing and contrasting; giving advice; talking about preferences; talking about plans; arguing pros and cons	Simple present; verb + infinitive; adverbs of frequency	Allocate time; manage self
3	Home and Neighborhood: community problems; neighborhood; neighborhood security	Security guards	Offers, requests, and warnings; discussing problems	*There is, there are, there was, there were*; past regular and irregular verbs; prepositions of location	Solve problems; teach others
4	Employment and Opportunity: success and successful people in the United States; successful immigrant Americans	Teamwork and leading a group	Asking for and giving information	Simple past in yes/no questions and negative statements, past time expressions	Exercise leadership; monitor and correct performance; participate as a member of a team
5	Healthy Living: health, exercise, risk factors for heart disease; missing work because of illness	U.S. concerns about dieting and losing weight	Comparing and contrasting; asking for and giving advice	Direct object pronouns, future with *going to*, count and noncount nouns	Acquire and evaluate information; make decisions
6	Home and Neighborhood: renting an apartment; daycare; mortgage rates; renting vs. buying	Operating a home daycare business	Asking for and giving information	*How much/how many*; future with *will*; wh-question words	Serve clients or customers; negotiate and arrive at decisions; evaluate information and make decisions
7	Transportation and Travel: transportation; accidents and accident reports; trains and buses; buying a car	Driving rules and responsibilities	Asking for and giving directions; expressing necessity; reporting something	*Need to, have to*; present continuous; *could* and *would* for requests	Allocate money; demonstrate responsibilities
8	Community Services: libraries and community services; getting a library card; freedom of speech	Freedom of speech	Telling what one should and shouldn't do; apologizing	*Should* and *shouldn't*; demonstrative pronouns; demonstrative adjectives	Select technology; apply technology to task; apply problem solving skills
9	Employment and Opportunity: job search; interview tips; what employers want of new employees	Job search, interview tips; what employers want of new employees	Expressing ability and inability; making suggestions; giving advice	Meanings of *can* and *can't*; compound sentences; *must* and *must not, must* and *have to*	Organize and maintain information; sociability
10	Consumer Economics: shopping; discounts; bargains	Using coupons to save money	Complimenting; comparing and contrasting	Indirect objects; comparative adjectives; meanings of *could* and *couldn't*	Allocate money; participate as a member of a team

Scope and Sequence: Book 3

Unit	Topics	Culture Focus	Functions	Grammar	SCANS Competencies
1	People and Machines: business machines; the Internet	Machines and where they are used	Explaining; expressing needs; making suggestions	Adverbial clauses with *because* and *so*; two-word verbs	Select technology: apply technology to a task
2	Arts and Entertainment: U.S. jazz; music and clubs	Music festivals in the United States	Expressing likes and dislikes; asking for and giving information	Verbs with reflexive pronouns; *each other*	Work with cultural diversity; social skills
3	Home and Neighborhood: decorating one's home; colors; weddings; jobs in construction and design	Cultural connotations of color	Expressing needs and desires; complimenting; describing	Order of adjectives; prepositions of location	Creative thinking; acquire and evaluate information
4	Healthy Living: health, fitness, insurance; good and bad habits; longevity	Americans living longer	Giving strong advice; expressing possibility; predicting consequences; expressing obligation and necessity	*Should, have to*, and *might; either . . . or; must, must not*	Acquire and evaluate information; monitor and correct performance
5	Human Relations: family, personal relationships; Larry King; child-care	Changes in the American family	Sympathizing; expressing surprise; expressing agreement and disagreement	Past participles; present perfect with *ever* and *always*; object pronouns	Social skills; interpret and communicate information; acquire and evaluate information
6	Consumer Economics: food, ingredients, cooking; regional food products	Regions and the foods they produce	Expressing dissatisfaction; talking about plans; sympathizing; making requests and commands	Inseparable two-word verbs; count and noncount nouns; quantifiers	Social skills; acquire and evaluate information
7	Employment and Opportunity: job benefits, days off; work and home responsibilities	Companies and benefits	Comparing and contrasting; explaining; asking for and giving information	Comparatives; superlatives	Decision making; acquire and evaluate information
8	History and Geography: immigration to the United States; ethnic groups	Ethnic groups and their occupations	Expressing worry; congratulating; complimenting; promising; predicting	Past continuous; past with *used to*; future with *will*	Interpret and communicate information; acquire and evaluate information; work with cultural diversity
9	Community Services: animals and people; pets; types of dogs	Pets in the United States	Making suggestions; asking for advice	*Ought to, should, have to, must*	Responsibility; acquire and evaluate information; creative thinking
10	Human Relations: nonverbal communication; shaking hands; relationships with co-workers	Shaking hands American style	Expressing unhappiness; expressing desires; expressing possibility; expressing obligation	Verbs with gerunds; sentences with *and*	Social skills; self-management; acquire and evaluate information

Scope and Sequence: Book 4

Unit	Topics	Culture Focus	Functions	Grammar	SCANS Competencies
1	Employment and Opportunity: networking; writing résumés and cover letters; preparing for interviews	Job skills for the future	Asking for and giving information; giving advice; introductions	Present perfect; present perfect continuous with *for* and *since*; simple past; present perfect; and present perfect continuous	Acquire and evaluate information; identify human resources; understand systems
2	Transportation and Travel: transportation announcements; vacation requests; accident reports; travel costs	U.S. emphasis on driving	Discussing problems; asking for and giving information; reporting something	Reported speech; present perfect; past perfect	Interpret and communicate information; think creatively; solve problems
3	Home and Neighborhood: natural disasters; volunteer organizations	Volunteer work	Asking for and giving information; offers, requests, and warnings	Passive voice; present conditional, conditional with *would*; conditional	Participate as a member of a team; organize and maintain information
4	Healthy Living: medical insurance coverage and claims; nutrition; non-traditional medicine	Alternative medicine	Asking for and giving information; comparing and contrasting	Gerunds and infinitives	Acquire and evaluate information; solve problems; self-manage
5	Employment and Opportunity: citizenship requirements, forms, and exam; undocumented immigrants	INS rules	Giving advice; expressing necessity; making suggestions; arguing pros and cons	Modals of advice and necessity; short answers, tag endings	Acquire and evaluate information; socialization, participate as a member of a team/negotiate
6	Arts and Entertainment: opinions; arts programs; family plans; entertainment expenses	Dance in different cultures	Comparing and contrasting; describing	Present participles as adjectives, past participles as adjectives	See things in the mind's eye; make decisions; teach others
7	History and Geography: small business; job retraining; overfishing; protecting natural resources	Water pollution	Talking about preferences arguing pros and cons	Relative clauses with *who*; relative clauses with *which* and *that*; word order in relative clauses	Interpret and communicate information; participate as member of a team
8	Consumer Economics: banking; small business loans; budgets; saving money in the United States and around the world	Employee benefits	Asking for and giving information; comparing and contrasting	Direct and indirect objects, embedded questions and embedded yes/no questions with infinitives	Acquire and evaluate information; identify and allocate resources (money); interpret and communicate information
9	Community Services: community resources; community college courses; single parents in the United States	Parenting strategies	Asking for and giving advice; asking for and giving information	Time clauses; clauses of cause and effect; clauses of opposition	Acquire and evaluate information; solve problems, reasoning (cause/effect and opposition)
10	People and Machines: telephone bills; using answering machines and voice mail; technology in school	Technology at home and work	Asking for and giving information; comparing and contrasting	Future conditional; phrasal verbs and separable phrasal verbs	Participate as a member of a team; understand systems; acquire and evaluate information

Introduction

Program Components and Philosophy

Contemporary English is a five-level interactive topic-based English-as-a-Second-Language series for adult learners ranging from the beginning-literacy level to the high-intermediate level. The series includes

- Student Books for classroom use
- Workbooks for independent use at home, in the classroom, or in a lab
- Audiocassettes for individual student, classroom, or lab use and
- Teacher's Manuals, with reproducible activity masters and unit progress checks for assessment. These materials were correlated from inception to the California Model Standards for Adult ESL Programs, the MELT Student Performance Levels, and the SCANS (Secretary's Commission on Achieving Necessary Skills) Competencies.

Unique among adult ESL series, *Contemporary English* presents high-interest topics as a framework for developing a wide variety of language, thinking, and life skills. In addition to focusing on listening, speaking, reading, and writing skills, *Contemporary English* integrates work on language structures; problem-solving, critical-thinking, and graphic-literacy skills; and—increasingly important—work-related skills.

Contemporary English empowers students to take charge of their learning and to develop strong communication skills for the real world. For example, each unit in Books 1–4 falls under one of the following broad topics: Home and Neighborhood, People and Machines, Employment and Opportunity, Human Relations, Consumer Economics, Community Services, Transportation and Travel, Healthy Living, History and Geography, and Arts and Entertainment. (The lowest-level book, *Contemporary English* Literacy, addresses all of these topics except History and Geography and Arts and Entertainment.) In short, the series addresses topics of interest and concern to adult learners.

Contemporary English presents engaging and meaningful situations that provide a context for grammar structures, listening activities, and an emphasis on the world of work. Within this framework each unit offers a wealth of pair and group activities, often with designated team roles, and frequent individual and group presentations to the class. This approach mirrors the team organization characteristic of today's workplace and reflects the recent influence on education of the Department of Labor's SCANS report.

Teaching Suggestions

In general, keep the following suggestions in mind when you introduce activities from this series.

1. Rather than direct the classroom, try to manage or facilitate learning and encourage your learners to take active roles, even at the lowest levels of instruction.

2. Model activities before learners do them so that learners have a clear idea of how to work with a partner or a group.

3. Whenever possible, use students or classroom objects and people in your models. For example, say, "I am a teacher" or "She is a student." Move around the class and use gestures to convey meaning.

4. Review the directions orally and ask learners if they have questions.

5. Monitor learners as they do the activities.

6. Provide follow-up activities in some of these ways:
   - When appropriate, post learners' work on the classroom walls for them to read.
   - Have pairs or small groups share role-played conversations with the rest of the class.
   - From time to time, have learners informally reflect on their participation by asking themselves questions such as these: "How well did I understand the activity? Was I a good listener? How much did I participate?"

As you progress through the units, always try to consider the book as a meaningful whole. Whenever possible, review aspects of content, language, vocabulary, and workplace skills, and incorporate them into each new unit. In this way, the process of recycling—a strong feature of this series—can be customized to meet the needs of your class.

General extension activities can be used in all units. In Book 1 you can use TPR (Total Physical Response) activities quite successfully as extension. True role-playing can be used especially from Book 2 on up. Improvisation can be used in Books 3 and 4. Strip stories can be created from the readings at all levels. Higher-level students can be asked to read or find newspaper and magazine articles related to unit topics. And for classrooms or programs with technological capability, the Internet, word-processing, database, and even spreadsheet activities related to series topics—such as job-search and citizenship issues—can be highly motivating and also practical, as students can list this experience for employers in their job-skills summary.

Use of monolingual English dictionaries is appropriate in Books 3 and 4, and bilingual native-language dictionaries can be used at all levels.

Dictations

You may want to do a dictation activity every time the class meets. Dictation is a good way to practice several English skills simultaneously, as learners listen, write, and read sentences in English. You can choose two sentences from one of the Scenes or a short section from one of the readings. Follow these steps.

1. Tell learners to listen to the first sentence but not write it.
2. Repeat the sentence. Tell learners how many words are in it.
3. Give learners time to write the sentence.
4. Repeat the sentence again if needed.
5. Show learners where to find the sentence in the book.

Language Experience Stories

At the lower levels of the series, you may also want to use learner-generated language experience stories in your teaching approach. If you are not yet comfortable using language experience stories as a whole-class activity, the following steps may be helpful:

1. Ask the class to look at a photo or illustration related to the content of the unit.
2. Have learners talk about the visual.
3. Write what they say.
4. Read their words to them.
5. Ask if they want to make any changes or corrections, but keep the emphasis on the connection between spoken and written language, not on correct grammar.
6. Read the story aloud while learners follow along.

7. Point to words and sentences and have learners read them to you.

8. Have learners practice reading the story as many times as they show interest in doing so.

Journal Writing

You may want to have higher-level students keep journals to improve their written English. If you have not monitored journal writing before, try following these suggestions:

1. Give learners a formal or informal schedule on which you will review the journals.

2. Tell them to write about anything they are interested in learning about that day or week. Low-level students or those who have little practice writing may need to write just one sentence every day at the end of class.

3. After reading each journal, write several sentences or questions about the entries.

4. Don't make corrections unless the individual learner asks you to do so.

5. Discuss journal entries with their student authors.

Bringing the World to the Classroom

1. Ask learners to look in magazines or newspapers for stories related to the unit. An alternative is to bring periodicals to class yourself and look through them together.

2. Listen to the radio or television for stories about topics related to those in the units. Ask learners if they have heard or seen the stories.

3. Talk about the stories in class and relate them to the unit.

Always encourage learners to take active roles, even at the lowest levels of instruction. One way in which you can move learning in a more active direction is to have students ask the questions provided in the unit-specific notes in this Teacher's Manual. You can write the questions on 3 x 5 inch index cards, hand them to students, and let them direct their own and one another's learning. Higher-level students can add a question of their own to the cards, and students can exchange cards. The possibilities for encouraging active learning with *Contemporary English* are unlimited.

Graphic Organizers

These useful tools for organizing individual or collective thinking and writing play a central role in *Contemporary English*. Graphic organizers such as Venn diagrams, idea maps, T-charts, and Johari windows can be used successfully in the learning process. Graphic organizers are particularly helpful in developing higher-level thinking skills, and the visual aspect of these tools makes them ideal for visual learners.

Even among experienced teachers and teacher trainers, there is surprising variation among terms used to identify certain procedures and techniques for language learning, so the following definitions may be useful to you in working with graphic organizers. Although you may already be familiar with the definitions, consider presenting them to your class and explaining that you will be using certain organizers throughout the term. In the student materials themselves, efforts have been made to provide very brief definitions in context so that students will feel comfortable with the designated organizers for their level even when working independently.

Johari window. A square divided into four parts; a four-paned window. While Joharis can, of course, compare four different things, they are most commonly used to compare and contrast two things in this way:

> panel 1: A has/does/etc. this

> panel 2: B has/does/etc. this

> panel 3: Both A and B have/do/etc. this

> panel 4: Neither A nor B has/does/etc. this

T-chart. A two-column chart (in the form of a T), used to compare or contrast.

Venn diagram. Two overlapping circles, also used to compare and contrast. Properties of two things or concepts are written in the outer portions of the circles. In the overlapping section, shared properties are written.

Idea map. An organizer used to brainstorm ideas and gather information. The map has a central circle with a topic word, phrase, or sentence and connected circles surrounding it in which related or subordinate ideas or examples are written.

Time line. Even at the lowest levels of English instruction, the time line is a useful tool for teaching sequencing skills. As your students do the time line activities related to the content of their books and workbooks, you can guide them, whenever appropriate, to create their own time lines for different stages of their lives. This process involves gathering data and subsequently organizing it and presenting it to an audience.

The Student Book

Before you begin the first **Scene,** discuss—or explain with words and gestures if necessary—the meaning of the title, which can be a springboard to understanding the central issues. You also may wish to bring in photos, illustrations, and/or realia that illustrate the content and the concept. At more advanced levels, ask students themselves to predict what the unit is going to be about.

Ask questions that encourage students to contribute general information and personal information related to the topic (for example, "Fatima, do many people have big families in your country? Juan, do you have brothers?").

Write some of the questions and answers on the board or provide a handout.

You may wish to have students ask and answer some of the same questions in pairs.

Scenes

Each unit is divided into two parts, each of which begins with a **Scene** that presents, in comic-strip format, incidents from the lives of newcomers to the United States or aspects of U.S. culture that students encounter regularly. Lively, humorous, and dramatic, the **Scenes** engage students in the unit topics—usually by presenting typical problems in the lives of average people. A series of discussion questions proceeds from factual comprehension of the **Scene** to personalization and, in Books 3 and 4, problem solving. For example, at the highest level the sequence is *Facts* (comprehension questions), *Feelings* (inference), *And You?* (application), *Comparisons* (often between the students' native countries and the United States), and, finally, the *Action* problem-solving questions—for example, *What should ___ do?*

Here are some techniques to enhance class work for each **Scene** with lower-level learners:

1. Write the conversation on the board.

2. Read or play each line of the conversation twice and ask the class to repeat it. Whenever possible, emphasize a holistic approach. In other words, try to have learners deal with whole chunks of language, rather than breaking language down word by word.

3. Read the language that learners have difficulty pronouncing and ask them to repeat words and phrases as a class as often as necessary. As soon as pronunciation improves, work with repetition of the entire line again.

4. Ask individual students to repeat the line.

5. Have students do a final choral repetition. Then move to the next line.

6. As each new line is practiced, add it to the previously learned section of the Scene. Continue this way until students can repeat the entire dialogue. At higher levels you may wish to have learners read the cartoon in groups of twos or threes.

7. Review new or difficult vocabulary.

8. Say the words and have learners repeat them.

9. Elicit definitions of the words. Check comprehension. If students cannot define the words, you can provide definitions or examples.

10 Extend the **Scene** by doing some or all of the following activities:

- Have learners spell the words (on the board or aloud).

- Use the words in two or three sentences.

- Ask learners to use the words in sentences.

- Have students practice in pairs as you move around the classroom, checking pronunciation.

- Have learners take roles and read the dialogue aloud. Allow several pairs or groups of students to present each **Scene** for the class.

- Have partners take turns dictating the conversations. Student A can dictate while Student B writes the conversation in his or her ESL notebook.

- Write three to five sentences on small paper strips and hand these to individual learners. When prompted, each learner can read his or her sentence. You can then write each on the board or on an overhead transparency. Lower-level classes can copy the sentences. The class can then order the sentences chronologically by assigning a number to each one.

- Read a summary of the **Scene.** Then write it on the board or an overhead transparency, or provide it on a handout. Remove the summary and have learners write their own.

- After learners answer the questions under the **Scene**, have each one write one or two additional questions to ask other learners.

- Have students retell the story and write about the pictures in their own words.

These activities are particularly useful with multilevel classes. The **Scenes** introduce students to the topic of the unit, give them a context for the grammar, get them interested and involved in the story, and build a context for the unit.

Sound Bites

After each opening **Scene** comes **Sound Bites,** a focused listening task that includes prelistening and postlistening work. **Sound Bites** presents target content and language structures through lively conversations and other samples of natural speech, such as telephone answering-machine messages and transportation announcements.

For any **Sound Bites** activity, you can follow these steps:

1. Read the directions aloud.

2. Model the directions.

3. Tell students what kind of conversations or passages they will listen to.

4. Read or play the tape for each individual **Sound Bites** item several times. Speak at a normal speed. Remember that learners don't need to understand every word to get meaning.

5. Model the appropriate written response.

6. Let students listen as often as they want.

At lower levels let students direct their learning by frequently asking them questions such as "Do you need to listen again?" and teaching them to ask clarification questions such as "Can you repeat number six?" At higher levels you may wish to have students take notes as they listen.

You can provide repeated active-listening experiences for all levels of students by assigning a different focus for each one. For example, play **Sound Bites** the first time and ask students, "Have you heard anything like this before? Where were you?" Then play the tape again and have students listen for vocabulary. A third time they can listen for something else—perhaps to complete the task or to listen for specific questions you provide, such as "What kind of person is Jerry?" Encourage students to compare answers. As an extension activity, later in the unit, you may wish to make the **Sound Bites** into a cloze exercise, for example, by leaving out the examples of the grammar point throughout.

Vocabulary Prompts, Your Turn, and In Your Experience

Vocabulary Prompts, Your Turn, and **In Your Experience** occur within the units at the point of need, rather than in a fixed or unvarying part of each unit. **Vocabulary Prompts,** for example, serves to isolate challenging vocabulary before a listening or reading task. **Your Turn,** a follow-up to reading, listening, or structure practice, serves as a participatory task. **In Your Experience,** an activity drawing on students' prior knowledge and personal lives, allows learners to personalize the topics and relate them to their own experience.

In Book 1, before students actually open their books to one of these vocabulary sections, you may want to prepare them by doing the following:

1. Show related pictures, maps, and realia.

2. Provide clear pronunciation models and ask students to repeat each word or term several times.

3. Provide additional explanations and examples as needed and use people and objects in the classroom whenever possible.

4. Finally, preview the **Sound Bites** tape and ask learners to listen for the words in the **Vocabulary Prompts** box.

A way to maximize learners' opportunities to practice oral communication in the **Your Turn** and **In Your Experience** sections is to use three-way interviews. These proceed in the following way: Students 1 and 2 talk to each other; Students 3 and 4 talk to each other. Then 1 and 3 talk, and 2 and 4 talk. Finally, 1 and 4 talk, and 2 and 3 talk. You can then assign all students with one number to report their results to the class. This procedure allows everybody plenty of opportunities to talk.

Spotlight

Throughout *Contemporary English*, grammar structures are first contextualized in the **Scenes** and listening activities, and then presented, practiced, and applied on follow-up **Spotlight** pages. Appearing two to four times in each unit, the **Spotlight** pages model target structures in contexts related to the unit topic. Special **Spotlight** feature boxes present the target structures schematically and provide brief, straightforward explanations when necessary. Exercises following the structure presentations allow students to manipulate the structures in meaningful contexts, such as stories or real-life situations. **Spotlight** pages usually end with a **Your Turn** and/or an **In Your Experience** activity providing communicative application of the new structures.

To present the **Spotlight** structures most effectively to learners using Books 1 and 2 of the series, try the following sequence of steps:

1. Ask questions that either lead into the target structures or contain the target structures. For example, to lead into the target structures, you can ask questions that would normally take an answer with the target structure. You can then elicit the correct structure or, if students are unable to produce it, provide a sentence containing the structure. In this way, you will establish an appropriate context for the target structure from the beginning.

2. Guide students through the language forms in the **Spotlight** box.

3. Elicit and answer any questions learners may have.

4. Provide oral practice for correct pronunciation of the sentences containing the forms.

5. Read any rules that follow the example sentences, and then return to the sentences to demonstrate those rules.

With learners using Books 3 and 4, the following suggestions may help:

1. Ask questions that either lead into the target structures or contain the target structures. For example, to lead into the target structures, you can ask questions that would normally take an answer with the target structure. You can then elicit the correct structure or, if students are unable to produce it, provide a sentence containing the structure. In this way, you will establish an appropriate context for the target structure from the beginning.

2. After you have elicited or provided several examples of the target structure, try to elicit rules from learners. Many may have encountered the structures before or may actually have studied them formally.

3. You may wish to put sentences on the board for students to complete with the target structures. You can continue in this way until the class begins to get a feeling for the new structure.

4. Draw two faces. Write a conversation in speech bubbles for them but leave blanks. Say, "Just shout out the missing part. What should it be?" (For example, "I want to _____." or "I need to _____.")

5. Have students open their books and look at the **Spotlight** box. Depending on the level and ability of the class, have students read silently, prompt different learners to read parts of the box, or read to learners.

6. Ask, "Do you have questions?" If no one has a question, ask students to do the exercises as suggested in the sections that follow.

Spotlight Exercises

Follow these steps with the **Spotlight** exercises:

1. Whenever possible, have learners do the exercises with a partner or a small group. This allows for interaction and speaking practice. Assign partners or, if the class interacts well without prompting, allow students to choose their partners. If some learners prefer to work alone, at least have them check their answers with a partner.
2. Read the exercise directions aloud to students and point out the completed example.
3. Model the activity and ask if learners understand.
4. Check answers by asking one student from each pair to read that pair's sentences to the class.
5. Allow for differences. Some students may be especially interested in learning forms and may want you to create charts of language forms on the board, on an overhead transparency, or on handouts.

Person to Person

Listening and speaking skills are developed further in the **Person to Person** activities, which present recorded two-person conversations exploring the unit topics in natural, colloquial language. Students listen to conversations, practice them, and work in pairs to complete a final open-ended dialogue. Students can then present their new conversations to the class.

Have students listen first, rather than read, in order to focus on the meaning of each conversation. Read or play the tape for each conversation separately. Ask learners if you should repeat the conversations or replay the tape. Ask some general questions (such as "Who are the speakers?") to check comprehension. Have learners practice words and phrases after you. You may wish to avoid having them read at this point.

Have students practice each conversation in pairs. Then ask for volunteers to role-play each conversation. Reluctant students will be more likely to participate after eager volunteers have done so.

Some students may not want to do the final, creative conversation, and it is better not to force the issue. Instead, you may wish to have learners again volunteer to perform conversations for the class.

Try to check the conversations learners create before they present them to the class so that errors are not internalized by listeners. Of course, even after you check the conversations, presentations will quite likely have some errors, but resist the temptation to correct as learners speak. A better approach is to take notes on the errors and provide these to students later, along with positive comments on their performances.

To extend the **Person to Person** activities, have learners record their conversations on an audiocassette player. Then play all the conversations for the class. Also, you may wish to have learners write their final conversation. You can then put all the papers into a box and ask each pair of learners to draw out a conversation, practice it, and perform it for the class. If appropriate, ask listeners to try to guess the authors of each conversation based on content clues.

Reading for Real

Contemporary English helps students develop their reading skills and become motivated readers of English through **Reading for Real**, a page in each unit that provides stimulating authentic or adapted texts. With passages and realia that typically relate directly to the lives of characters in the **Scenes, Reading for Real** includes such real-life documents as a winning job résumé, instructions for office voice mail, biographies of real people, advice from the local police, and listings of music festivals around the country. Follow-up activities (such as **Your Turn** and **In Your Experience**) extend and personalize the reading.

Before beginning **Reading for Real,** try the following:

1. Prepare students by asking them to look at the pictures and the realia on the page.
2. Have them glance at the reading and ask questions such as the following:
   - What is this? (a bill? a résumé?)
   - Have you ever seen anything like this before?
   - Have you ever gotten one of these?
   - How does it relate to what we've been doing?
   - Why are you looking at this?
   - What will you read to find out?

Continue with the following steps:

Books 1 and 2

1. Read the text aloud.
2. Check students' comprehension.
3. Encourage the class to talk about the topic by asking questions.
4. Record ideas on the board or a flipchart.

Books 3 and 4

1. Ask learners to scan for specific pieces of information. With less advanced students you may wish just to call out words and have students circle them.
2. Tell students to read silently without stopping.
3. After they read, ask them to check a maximum of three words they don't know. Tell them you will talk about the words as a class later.
4. Emphasize to learners that things can—and should—be read more than once. Tell them that even the best readers don't remember everything the first time and that those readers reread difficult sections automatically.
5. Finally, stress that they don't have to worry about not being able to pronounce all the words at the beginning.
6. After **Reading for Real, Your Turn,** and **In Your Experience,** extend and personalize the reading. For example, after reading a brief résumé prepared by one character, students, with the help of a partner, use the model provided to write their own résumés. Partners then meet with another pair, exchange résumés, and make suggestions or corrections.

Culture Corner

Culture Corner provides further work on reading skills by focusing on the useful inside information about U.S. life that students love. Presented as brief readings typically paired with charts, graphics, or artwork, **Culture Corner** gives students the information they need to adapt to a culture that can often be confusing and difficult to understand. Interactive follow-up activities help students integrate cultural knowledge with their language skills.

The following steps will be useful in implementing **Culture Corner:**

1. Have students look at the illustration or diagram.

2. Ask questions that encourage thoughtful guessing. If some students are advanced enough to ask others questions, encourage them to do so.

3. Have learners read the short text silently on their own.

4. When students finish, read the text aloud to them and check their comprehension.

5. Ask learners to create one or two questions about the text and ask a partner those questions.

6. If possible, have the pairs of students write their questions and answers.

As an extension activity for the **Culture Corner,** you may wish to do the following, at least in some units: Draw a simple T-chart or Venn diagram on the board or distribute copies of one of these generic organizer masters as a handout. Then ask students to compare some aspect of life in the United States to life in their native countries.

Scene 2

The second half of the unit begins with a second **Scene,** which usually reintroduces at least one character from the previous **Scene.** This is followed by a second, smaller **Sound Bites** that recycles the **Scene's** language and content. Next comes one or more **Spotlight** pages.

To recycle language effectively, before you start work on Scene 2, revisit the first page of the unit and retell the story in the first **Scene.** This recycling is especially important in situations where attendance is sporadic or where open-entry/open-exit policies are common practice.

Based on this rereading, ask learners to make predictions about **Scene 2.** Read the speech bubbles, look at the pictures, and follow the steps suggested for **Scene 1** on pages xii and xiii.

The second, smaller **Sound Bites** (which appears in Books 2–4) recycles the language and content of **Scene 2.** It differs from the first **Sound Bites,** which serves as an initial introduction of the unit topic in that there are no picture cues and students need to take notes on what they hear.

Get Graphic

Graphic literacy is the focus of **Get Graphic,** a feature that offers practice in reading charts, graphs, diagrams, and time lines—skills that are crucial in the workplace and for preparing for the GED. **Get Graphic** provides high-interest stimuli related to the unit topics and characters while it incorporates or recycles target language structures. A typical feature of this page is a follow-up activity in which learners develop their own simple graphs or charts and share them with partners or groups. The activities on this page help students learn to read, interpret, and use information in a graphic format.

Follow the steps below to ensure learners' success with chart and graph work:

1. Try to introduce the activity through something in the classroom. For example, if the graphic in the student book is a pie graph, use the board or an overhead transparency to draw a very simple pie graph for the class population with information about students from different countries, students' native languages, different eye colors, and so on. Explain what the graph is and what it shows.

2. Check students' comprehension by asking if there are questions. Also, ask questions about the information on the graph. If students demonstrate comprehension, move into the graph in the book.

3. Have students quickly look at the graph. Ask, "What is this? What is the title? What do the numbers on the sides mean?"

4. Ask if students have seen a graph like this before and, if so, where? Was it at work? in a newspaper or magazine? in a math class?

5. You may wish to discuss and demonstrate the meaning of words such as *axis, fraction, decimal,* and *time line.*

6. Finally, read the directions, point out any examples, and model the activity.

7. Encourage work in pairs and small groups. If students work alone, try to have them check their answers with a partner or a small group.

Issues and Answers

Problem-solving and critical-thinking skills are developed further in **Issues and Answers.** This feature typically presents two opinions—often in direct opposition—in formats such as advice columns or letters to the editor. **Issues and Answers** contains short, humorous texts with views of U.S. life from a variety of perspectives, including those of immigrants and their "cultural advisors"—the experts who help to orient the newcomers as they bridge the gap between their native and adopted countries.

Here are some ways to implement **Issues and Answers:**

1. Before your students read, have copies of newspaper advice columns available for them to look at.

2. Prepare them for the reading by pointing out the column format. Show them that in the advice-column type of **Issues and Answers** found in some units of their books, the letter on the left asks a question that the letter on the right answers.

3. Encourage silent reading first because **Issues and Answers** is a reading activity. With lower-level students follow the silent reading by reading the text aloud.

4. Check students' comprehension by asking questions.

5. Have a class discussion about the topic.

6. Record students' ideas on the board or on a flipchart.

Wrap-Up and Think About Learning

In Books 2–4 the last page of each unit contains a **Wrap-Up,** a project in which students use a graphic organizer such as a T-chart, a Venn diagram, an idea map, or a time line to brainstorm and organize ideas and then talk or write in a group. Following **Wrap-Up** is the self-assessment activity **Think About Learning,** a final reflection task that asks students to evaluate the quality of their own learning on the major content points, life skills, and language structures in the unit. Students can thus assess what they have learned and provide feedback to the teacher, all of which helps to build a learner-centered classroom.

At the very end of each unit in Book 1 is **Think About Learning.** In every even-numbered unit of Book 1, this activity follows **Wrap-Up.** In odd-numbered units **Think About Learning** follows **Issues and Answers.** In each case, **Think About Learning** provides a way for students to assess what they have learned and provide feedback to the teacher, all of which helps build a learner-centered classroom.

Before administering the unit assessment, or **Progress Check,** always take time to study learners' responses to **Think About Learning** and systematically review points that need further work, ideally working both with the whole class and with individual students or small groups.

Unit Follow-up

After learners have recorded their progress, you may wish to talk about the following in class:

- what students thought was the most important thing they learned in the unit
- what part of the unit they enjoyed most
- other situations in which they could use the same skills and strategies
- other previously mastered skills and strategies that could relate to the content of the unit just studied

In the beginning some of this may be difficult for students. Remind them to continue using previously introduced strategies and skills as they add new ones. As they progress through the book, they will expand their repertory of learning strategies.

Finally, before moving to a new unit, ask learners if they would like to do anything different the next time. Try to respect these wishes by tailoring the instruction for your learners, thus giving them a real sense of directing their own learning. The learning process will be more dynamic if these possibilities for building on experience and creating positive change can flourish in the classroom.

The Workbooks

The *Contemporary English* Workbooks are designed for individual independent study as well as for classroom work. In the Workbooks, as in the Student Books, a predictable sequence is maintained.

For ease of use, the essential information in the **Spotlight** boxes of the Student Books is reproduced in the Workbooks. Each **Spotlight** is followed by a series of contextualized practice exercises, progressing from simple fill-ins to more challenging activities that ask students to use the target structures as they write answers to real-life questions about themselves. Answers to all Workbook activities can be found in the Teacher's Manual.

The **Read, Think, and Write** pages at the end of each Workbook unit for Books 2–4 synthesize skills presented and practiced in the unit in an engaging multistage activity. The reading is supported by pre- and postreading questions. After the reading, one or two activities ask learners to organize the information, usually with the same type of graphic organizer used in **Wrap-Up** in the Student Book. The final problem-solving activity challenges learners to apply the content to their own lives. Each unit closes with a brief questionnaire, similar to **Think About Learning** in the Student Book, in which students note what was most enjoyable and helpful in the Workbook.

Using a Problem-Posing Approach

Contemporary English stresses problem-solving and critical-thinking skills. Many teachers, however, may want to go beyond this framework to use a problem-posing approach, which focuses specifically on the lives of students and their own special concerns. While all of the topics in *Contemporary English* are applied to students' lives, using problem posing may help to make the connection with students' real concerns even stronger. The questions on the first page of each unit are an ideal place to begin problem posing, which involves the three following stages:

1. listening for students' concerns and issues
2. having a dialogue in which the class thinks about these issues
3. thinking about changes that people can make in their situations and suggesting a course of action

Key to this whole process is to make the discussion as learner centered as possible, so that students' issues and concerns—rather than the hypothetical or imaginary situations of characters in the text—become the focus of discussion. The text, however, can serve as a springboard for exploring students' problems since it brings into focus situations in which students and newcomers to the United States typically find themselves. Of course, students' concerns will often go beyond the context of life in the United States; and if you use problem posing, you will want to explore all of these concerns, to the extent that students find them important.

The Audiocassettes

All key listening components of each unit are available on audiocassette. These include the **Scenes**, **Sound Bites**, **Person to Person** conversations, and the **Listen** component of the **Progress Check.**

The Teacher's Manuals

The Teacher's Manuals give teachers additional tools to enhance learning and create an active, dynamic classroom. These include the general Introduction you are now reading for suggestions on using the approach successfully as well as unit-specific pages with teacher-friendly suggestions for preparing for, presenting, and extending activities. For ease of use, the unit-specific directions for a particular activity refer to a page of the general suggestions in this introductory unit. Many content questions that you can ask students at various points in the unit (to check comprehension and encourage application and synthesis) are also included in the unit-specific notes.

In addition, the Teacher's Manuals contain a variety of suggestions for adapting activities to the needs of multilevel classes. These suggestions are listed as Options, and they are signalled in the text by the following icon, placed in the margin:

At the end of this general introduction are two special sections: "Maximizing Results in the Multilevel Classroom" and "Creating a Work-Oriented Classroom." Written by teachers whose classroom and administrative experience makes them experts in those issues, these sections provide valuable information on using *Contemporary English* effectively in a variety of classroom settings.

Assessment

Flexible two-page **Progress Checks** allow a program or teacher to assess learning systematically. The four sections of these tests—**Speak or Write, Listen, Language Structures,** and **Content**—can be evaluated quickly to determine readiness to move to the next unit. The **Progress Checks** are largely self-explanatory and need no special instructions here apart from a word of caution on the **Listen** section. It is best not to read the listening script slowly to accommodate learners' developing listening skills. Rather, it is better to read each passage two or three times—but always at a normal rate of speed.

Activity Masters

Two reproducible **Activity Masters** extend each unit's learning still further. One is an interactive activity—a strip story, game, sequencing activity, or information gap—that practices language structures and reinforces content. This master can also be effective as a team-building, cooperative-learning activity. The other master— usually an additional reading or a graphic literacy activity to be completed individually or in pair or team situations— can also be used as part of the **Progress Check.**

Here are a few practical classroom management suggestions for using the **Activity Masters:**

1. Explain the general purpose of the handouts to learners. Tell them that the hand-outs will give them more language and vocabulary practice and allow them to share information and ideas with other learners.

2. If possible, copy the handouts on card stock so that they will be more durable and will last longer.

3. Store the masters in labeled envelopes or in a small standing or hanging file.

4. Handouts that need to be cut have dotted lines and scissors icons. Rather than cut apart your masters, whenever possible, have learners cut their individual copies. This will give them a more active role, and it will decrease your preparation time.

An additional tool for each unit is the Workbook Answers page, also on a reproducible master so that you can copy it for students if you wish them to check their own homework or one another's.

Maximizing Results in the Multilevel Classroom

by Elizabeth Minicz, Harper College, Palatine, Illinois

Everyone who has taught adult ESL classes is aware of the phenomenon of multi-level classes. The causes—among which are varying levels of education, disparate skill development, and open-enrollment policies—are further complicated by other factors which affect language learning, such as hemispheric dominance, personality, and sensory modality preference. Given all the challenges of a multilevel class envi-ronment, can ESL teachers rise above them to teach effectively and even enjoy the process? The answer is a resounding yes—if they have some practical tips and tools to help them perform the job.

First, recognize and accept the fact that you cannot always be all things to all stu-dents. That said, allow yourself the freedom to experiment with the techniques, methods, or "tricks of the trade" that experienced multilevel teachers discover through trial and error, and give yourself permission to fail from time to time. Some years ago, Tom Peters cautioned people in the business world to make mistakes quickly. This is sound advice for ESL teachers too; if something isn't working, try something else—immediately!

Below are some tried and true ways for you to use the realities of multilevel classes to your advantage. As you read them, you may have an occasional "Aha!" reac-tion—Aha, I can do that! Aha, I've done that! Aha, so that's why that works! In the end, there really is no magic answer to what to do about multilevel classes. You need to decide what works best for you, feels most comfortable, and best promotes learning. These things will always vary from teacher to teacher and class to class. Here are several approaches you should consider in using your students' variety of abilities to advantage.

Approach 1: Use a Variety of Grouping Strategies

How are grouping strategies in multilevel classes different from grouping strategies in homogeneous classes? Actually, the techniques are the same, but the purpose or intent is different. Using various grouping strategies in any class enhances learners' opportunities for practice. In multilevel classes, however, variations on grouping structures allow you to manage learner differences and abilities better. For example, separating learners according to language groups is a general grouping strategy, as are separating by gender, age, or interest. In multilevel classes, learners' abilities—which may vary according to the skill area targeted—also determine groupings. In multilevel classes, higher-level learners may be grouped together for one activity, and in another activity they may be grouped with lower-level learners.

In multilevel classes, whole-class activities can help learners develop a sense of community as they help one another succeed. They foster the "We're all in this together" feeling that temporarily overcomes individual differences. In addition, whole-class activities are confidence builders. Shy or timid learners can watch, listen, and "silently practice" until they feel comfortable participating more actively. More assertive learners can serve as role models, mentors, or tutors.

Despite these advantages of whole-class activities, if you always keep your class together, you can "miss" two-thirds of your learners because the activities are often too easy for one-third and too difficult for another third. It is important, then, to plan whole-class activities in which everyone can participate according to their individual abilities and to follow up with individual, pair, and group practice opportunities.

In *Contemporary English,* for example, the whole class looks at the pictures in a **Scene,** listens to **Sound Bites,** or reads silently. Such activities are followed by pair or group work, subsequent debriefing for the whole class, and, later, workbook activities completed at home or, if time permits, individually in class. Although in the **Scene** or **Sound Bites** all learners receive the same stimulus, individual responses will vary according to ability.

You will want to vary the pairings or groupings of learners from unit to unit, page to page, class session to class session. In homogeneous classrooms the purpose of varying groupings is simply to "mix up" the learners to avoid predictability and routine. In multilevel classes the purpose is to accommodate learner ability differences. Less able learners should have ample opportunity to work with more able learners, but not all the time!

Think through the purpose of pairings or groupings before directing your learners to work together. Arranging by categories or by assigning numbers or colors is common practice in both homogeneous and multilevel classrooms. But in homogeneous classrooms the results are random, while in multilevel classrooms you will want to determine the *who* and *why* of the groupings ahead of time. And sometimes you will want to let learners decide for themselves who they will work with.

If you are especially motivated or fond of challenges, you may have decided to use more than one level of *Contemporary English* in your class. If so, it's a good idea to begin each session with whole-class activities. Then plan to meet for 15 to 20 minutes with learners assigned to one level of the text while learners assigned to the other level(s) do pair, group, or individual work such as reading or writing. Finally, end by bringing all learners back together for a final whole-class activity. Although teaching from three levels of the series in your multilevel class is possible, two levels are undoubtedly more manageable.

Approach 2: Adapt the Textbook Pages for Different Proficiency Levels

This approach requires more planning time than Approach 1, in which—with the exception of using two or more levels of the series in the same class—the stimuli are the same for all learners, but responses vary according to individual abilities. In Approach 1 it is your standards that must change or adjust. However, in Approach 2 the stimulus itself varies according to ability level. This means you must create or adapt tasks according to the learners' proficiencies. For example, if learners have difficulty generating language to talk about the **Scenes,** you might pose a series of yes/no, either/or, or wh-questions for them to answer first orally and then in writing.

Another way to adjust the textbook materials up or down a notch is to look closely at the tasks learners are asked to do. For example, in some **Sound Bites** activities, learners listen and write a word or phrase. You may instead want give your lower-level learners several choices and ask them to circle or check the answers—since checking or circling are easier tasks than writing words or sentences. You can also limit the number of items lower-level learners hear or, conversely, increase the number of items for higher-level learners. When in doubt, let learners decide which level of activity to complete.

Here are some additional ways to modify activities for learners' differing abilities. For the **Person to Person** activities, you can assign more advanced learners all four conversations to practice and role-play. You can ask lower-level learners to listen to all four but have them choose only one to practice and role-play. Or higher-level learners may need the additional challenge of writing more than one original conversation in **Your Turn,** whereas lower-level learners may need to have the **Your Turn** structured more tightly, with specific questions and responses that you provide.

On the **Spotlight** pages have lower-level learners work together to complete the exercises but let higher-level learners work alone. Also, you may want them to act as your aides by helping you spot-check other learners' work.

As you teach from the series, you will discover on your own more ways to add to or reduce the language load for learners.

Approach 3: Structure Activities So That All Proficiency Levels Can Participate

Several kinds of activities can be particularly effective in multilevel classes. For example, you can provide learners with grammar practice by writing sentences and questions from **Spotlight, Reading for Real,** or **Issues and Answers** on sentence strips. Cut the strips into individual words, phrases, or clauses. Clip the words from each sentence together or put each sentence in a separate envelope. Give learners the sentences to unscramble according to their ability levels, with longer sentences going to higher-level learners and shorter ones to lower-level learners. These strips are worth the time you take to make them because they can be used over and over again. To increase the longevity of the strips, use cardboard or laminate them.

Activities involving sorting or categorizing and variations on vocabulary bingo are easy to prepare and provide meaningful practice for learners in multi-level classes. For each new unit copy **Activity Master 8-2** from the Book 1 Teacher's Manual, write the vocabulary words for the unit in the bingo squares and duplicate the page for learners' independent, pair, or group work. Then give learners scissors and have them cut out the word squares. Have them use these words for several sorts: words they know how to pronounce, words they know the meanings of, and words they can use in sentences. Otherwise, they can also use the words for alphabetizing practice. Or learners can scramble the words, put them in a pile, and take turns turning over a word, spelling it, or using it correctly in a sentence. The variations are endless.

Traditional vocabulary bingo uses an enjoyable format to provide learners with scanning practice. To play vocabulary bingo, use the same generic reproducible master mentioned above. Make the game challenging for different levels of learners by having higher-level learners pronounce, spell, and give definitions. Have lower-level learners simply say or spell the words.

In short, to maximize the effectiveness of *Contemporary English* in multilevel classes, you will need to be creative and flexible, and once you have found new ways to implement activities, share your innovations and successes with your colleagues!

Suggestions for Creating a Work-Oriented ESL Classroom

by Jan Jarrell, San Diego Community Colleges

In the last decade, modeling and practicing workplace tasks and situations have become increasingly important components of the adult ESL classroom. This trend—together with the related tendency toward increased accountability—has been prompted by three interrelated societal shifts: (1) welfare reform, (2) governmental pressure on educational institutions to link funding to outcomes, and (3) the changing nature of the workplace as described in the 1992 Secretary of Labor's Commission on Achieving Necessary Skills (SCANS) Report.

Brief Background and Description of SCANS

In the late 1980s the United States found itself playing catch-up with two booming economies: Germany's and Japan's. Comparisons of work practices in these three countries became commonplace, and as a result, many U.S. companies switched to Japanese-style management practices known as Total Quality Management (TQM). This approach coupled an emphasis on teamwork with quality control at the level of the individual employee. In response to these dramatic changes on shop floors as well as in boardrooms, the U.S. Secretary of Labor organized a national commission to identify what the new high performance workplace demanded from workers.

The fruit of this Commission was the SCANS report, which identified two tiers of essential workplace know-how: foundation skills and workplace competencies. Foundation skills include basic communication and math, as well as higher-level thinking, decision making and learning-how-to-learn skills. Personal qualities such as positive attitude, self esteem, and individual responsibility are also considered foundational. The higher-order workplace competencies include understanding and effectively using resources, technology, information, and systems. In addition, workers need effective interpersonal skills so they can work on teams, teach others, negotiate, serve customers and collaborate on the job with people from diverse backgrounds.

Continued study of workplace needs and trends since 1992 has confirmed the relevance, indeed the necessity, of integrating the SCANS competencies into the curriculum at every educational level. In order for ESL students to get and keep jobs even at the entry level, teaching the SCANS is no longer optional. Many ESL programs in states with significant second-language populations have partially or completely integrated SCANS competencies into their curricula to meet these new challenges.

Promoting Teamwork in the Classroom

Of all the SCANS competencies, learning to work effectively in teams is perhaps the most pivotal. Teamwork either directly or indirectly drives most of the other SCANS skills, and yet many ESL students have had very little experience working in teams in their own countries—either in the classroom or on the job.

The most obvious and pedagogically familiar way of promoting teamwork in the classroom is by integrating cooperative-learning structures into your lessons. According to Johnson, Johnson, and Smith (1991), cooperative learning can be distinguished from other pair or group work because it includes five key elements:

- **Positive Interdependence:** The success of each team member and that of the team in general depends upon the effectiveness of all team members. By promoting activities such as jigsaws, which, because no student has all the information, encourage sharing of knowledge and resources, and by assigning group roles, you can allow work in teams to emerge naturally in your classroom.
- **Individual Accountability:** Structure activities so that all students must contribute. Assessing both individuals and groups assures that all learners must participate.
- **Group Processing:** Regularly provide time for team reflection and evaluation.
- **Social Skills:** Through your explicit teaching, modeling, and reinforcement, your learners can learn to lead, build trust, make decisions, and deal with conflicts.
- **Face-to-Face Interaction:** If you physically arrange learners to facilitate active involvement with one another as they discuss, teach, encourage, solve problems and negotiate, you will enhance team spirit in your classroom. In cooperative learning jigsaw activities, for example, students master content in expert groups, and then return to home groups to teach the content they have learned and also to learn new content from their teammates. As such, positive interdependence, new social skills, and face-to-face interaction are built into the activity. Later, you can assess individuals on all the content and ask the different groups to evaluate the strengths and weaknesses of their group interaction. This allows you to build in the other two elements: individual accountability and group processing.

Team Roles

In the work-centered ESL classroom, you can assign individual team members workplace roles. For example, in a group task, each team can be comprised of a manager or leader, a secretary, a supply clerk and a timekeeper. The manager must make sure that everyone participates and may also present the group's findings to the whole class. The secretary records and reports the group's answers. The supply clerk makes sure each group member has the necessary materials and also collects and returns texts and papers at the end of the task. The timekeeper keeps the team on task by reminding members how much time remains for completing each activity. You can assign some or all of these roles on a class-by-class basis, or they can continue over a period of time. If students take roles for one or two months, you can periodically have "managers' meetings" in which assignments or problems can be discussed among the team managers who then report back to their respective teams.

Just like roles in the actual workplace, these roles are flexible, and the titles or jobs that learners assume can vary by project and possibly by geographical area or by preparation of learners for a particular sector of the economy. Having a secretary may be meaningful when many learners will be pursing an office skills track; similarly, the roles of recorder and reporter may be relevant for later involvement in community service projects. The choice of roles really depends upon you and the specifics of the business environment in your area.

Using the Reality of the Classroom

As SCANS and the workplace become more of an influence on classroom instruction, ESL instructors are often pleased to find that daily operations of the ESL classroom provide many opportunities for students to gain actual work experience. These tasks shift responsibility for the ESL class away from you and toward students themselves. In the workplace-centered classroom, you as the instructor become a facilitator rather than a performer or directive manager.

Classroom Management. You can assign many classroom maintenance tasks to student teams. Team members can check signatures on the sign-in sheet, welcome new students, erase boards, and straighten chairs. They can distribute, count, and collect textbooks and set up and test equipment such as overhead projectors and audiocassette recorders. You can ensure that this work is shared and completed by posting work schedules that indicate which teams are responsible for classroom maintenance tasks on any given week or day.

Students as Trainers. You may wish to identify classroom procedures that students can teach new members of the class. Examples of these procedures are explaining class rules, showing newcomers how to fill out registration cards, and demonstrating for them how to turn on a computer or load a software program. Peer revision is another excellent example of how all students can function as trainers for one another.

Solving Classroom Challenges. It's a fact that certain challenges arise all too often in the ESL classroom. Insufficient or uncomfortable work space, inappropriate first-language use in the classroom, teams' failure to fulfill their classroom duties—all of these may seem to be inevitable features of the adult ESL classroom. But instead of first defining and then solving these problems for learners, you can turn them into resources by involving your learners actively in the problem-solving process. School or classroom issues can be identified through an anonymous suggestion box or evaluation form. Then, in teams, students can list possible solutions to the problem, discuss positive and negative consequences of each solution, and finally choose one of these solutions, implement it, and evaluate the results either as individuals or in groups. After students implement the solution, the results can be evaluated either by individuals or in groups. As an alternative, try holding class meetings in which one representative from each team participates in a brainstorming session while the rest of the class observes and later offers feedback to the meeting participants.

Of course, other problems occur on an individual or personal level, and students need to be armed with strategies to handle them. When a technological problem such as a computer failure occurs, you can encourage students to troubleshoot by following an established procedure. You can also teach teams a process for dealing with interpersonal conflict without your intervention. For example, you can train students in a round-robin exercise procedure in which each team member has two minutes to talk without interruption about what he or she thinks the problem is. Sometimes simply airing problems in this safe way will significantly diffuse negative feelings. Following the round-robin, individual team members can also write their suggestions for solving the problem that has been identified, the team secretary or reporter can read the suggestions, and all members can then discuss them.

Emphasizing Accountability

Using Agendas. One easy way of keeping a class on track and modeling workplace procedures is to post an *agenda* at the start of each class. The agenda can be simply a numbered or bulleted list, or it also can indicate time frames for each activity. As each task is completed, you can check it off on the chalkboard and have students mark their ESL notebooks. At the end of class, you and your students can use the agenda to review what has been learned that day. Highlight any items that were not addressed and indicate when they will be included.

Checklists and Logs. Just as employees often need to account for how they spend time on the job, students can learn to monitor their own progress by marking checklists of skills, competencies, and objectives such as the **Think About Learning** chart at the end of each unit of the student books in this series. You may also wish to have students keep a daily or weekly log of what they study and accomplish.

Evaluation. Evaluation not only allows you to assess students' learning and interests, it also encourages critical thinking and decision making, two important SCANS skills. Evaluation can be formal or spontaneous, but it is an essential element of any work-centered classroom. It can be designed either to help the learner think about his or her own learning or to help the instructor quantify that learning.

On the formal end, instructors can prepare class evaluations in which students rate specific class activities on a scale. Students need to practice providing feedback because in the workplace they will often be asked to evaluate training they receive. Students can also grade themselves in mock performance self-appraisals. The **Think About Learning** component for each unit of this series can serve this purpose.

Less formally, you can also "check in" with students by simply distributing index cards at the end of a class period. On one side have students write what they found particularly helpful that day, and on the other side ask them to note what was unclear—or what they would like to study next. Finally, to raise students' own consciousness about the SCANS competencies, you may want to create a class poster of the SCANS using level-appropriate language or pictures. Then, at the end of each class, ask students which skills they practiced that day.

Classroom Incentives. Many businesses have an "Employee of the Month" award, typically for an exceptional worker, who gets his or her picture and biography posted on a special bulletin board. You can adopt this practice quite easily in the classroom by recognizing an individual student or a team each month. You may also want to present end-of-term certificates for attendance, punctuality, outstanding performance, "best suggestions," and so on. In addition, you can give letters of recommendation instead of, or in addition to, certificates. Students appreciate "to whom it may concern" letters that describe their strengths—such as being punctual or being a team player. These letters reaffirm the SCANS competencies, and students can actually use them to get jobs in the real world!

Workplace Language. All the suggestions outlined in this section provide students with learning experiences that can help them develop essential skills for the workplace. However, most of these strategies require systematic modeling and practice. For example, students need to be explicitly taught language to facilitate teamwork. They need to know how to agree and disagree politely, ask for repetition or clarification, and give instructions. For example, one of many employers' most frequent complaints is that employees do not let their supervisors know when they don't understand an instruction or procedure. As work-centered activities are implemented in the classroom, encourage students to use clarification strategies such as asking questions and paraphrasing instructions. By practicing the language that characterizes this new classroom environment, your learners will be actively preparing for the world of work. If you can help them to articulate these newfound skills to prospective employers, their chances of turning a job interview into a job offer can increase dramatically.

Organization of the Unit-Specific Materials in the Teacher's Manual

In the pages that follow, the teacher's material for each unit is arranged in the following order.

1. Overview

   A. Objectives

   • Skills and Structures

   • SCANS Competencies

   B. Realia

2. Unit-specific Activity Notes (with answers for student book exercises and indicators for when to use workbook pages)

3. Answers to **Progress Checks** and **Activity Masters**

4. Workbook Answers (provided on a separate, reproducible page)

5. Unit **Progress Checks**

6. Two reproducible **Activity Masters** (Note: teacher directions—in addition to the teacher and student directions that appear on the master itself—for some of the **Activity Masters** are provided in the teacher notes at the first point in the unit where the activity can be used).

Administering and Scoring the Placement Test

Allow 35 minutes for completion of the Placement Test. Use the Scoring Guide and the Answer Key below to score the tests.

Scoring Guide

Scores	Book	Level
0–3	Literacy	beginning literacy to literacy level
3–7	Book 1	low beginning level
8–17	Book 2	high beginning level
18–25	Book 3	low intermediate level
26–30	Book 4	high intermediate level

Answer Key

Part 1

1. d	2. c	3. b	4. a	5. c
6. b	7. c	8. a	9. a	10. b

Part 2

11. much	12. did
13. are	14. wasn't *or* was not
15. Where	16. were
17. Have	18. did
19. shouldn't *or* should not	20. am

Part 3

21. d	22. c	23. c	24. b	25. c
26. c	27. b	28. c	29. c	30. c

Name _____ Date _____

CONTEMPORARY ENGLISH PLACEMENT TEST

Examples

1. Complete the sentence. Circle the correct letter.

   What ___ you do in the mornings?

   a. do   b. does   c. are   d. am

2. Complete the conversation. Circle the correct letter.

   A: Are you from Algeria?

   B: Yes, I ___.

       a. is   b. are   c. am   d. be

Part I

1. Complete the conversation. Circle the correct letter.

   A: I took a vacation last week.

   B: Oh, really? ___

       a. Where did you went?   b. Where does you go?

       c. Where go you?   d. Where did you go?

2. Complete the conversation. Circle the correct letter.

   A: It was Alice's birthday last week.

   B: Oh, really? Did she get any interesting presents?

   A: Yes, ____

       a. Tom bought to her a beautiful lamp.

       b. Tom bought a beautiful lamp to her.

       c. Tom bought her a beautiful lamp.

       d. Tom bought a beautiful lamp her.

3. Complete the conversation. Circle the correct letter.

   A: Excuse me. ___ borrow your pen?

   B: Sure, no problem. Here you are.

       a. Do I   b. Could I

       c. Would I   d. Should I

4. Complete the conversation. Circle the correct letter.

   A: Can you help me? I need ___ box up there, but I can't reach it.

   B: Sure, I'll get it down for you.

       a. that   b. this   c. these   d. those

5. Complete the conversation. Circle the correct letter.

A: My car is getting really old.

B: I know. You ___ get a new one.

   a. would   b. may   c. should   d. need

6. Complete the sentence.

Have you ever ___ any repair work on your car?

   a. did   b. done   c. does   d. do

7. Complete the conversation. Circle the correct letter.

A: There are so many dresses here, and I like all of them. I don't know which one to choose.

B: Oh, I think this one is the ___

   a. better   . b. good   c. best   d. well.

8. Complete the conversation. Circle the correct letter.

A: Where are you from?

B: I'm from Spain.

A: Oh, I have never ___ to Spain.

   a. been   b. being   c. be   d. was

9. Complete the conversation. Circle the correct letter.

A: How is your daughter doing in school?

B: Oh, she's doing fine. In fact, she's ___ than many of the other kids in her class.

   a. better   b. best   c. good   d. well

10. Complete the conversation. Circle the correct letter.

A: You should stop ___ those boxes like that.

B: Why?

A: You'll hurt your back.

   a. to lift   b. lifting   c. lift   d. lifted

Part 2

Example

Complete the conversation. Fill in the blank.

A: _____*What*_____ is your name?

B: Maria.

11. Complete the conversation. Fill in the blank.

A: How _____ coffee do you want?

B: About a pound.

12. Complete the conversation. Fill in the blank.

A: Where _____ you live in your native country?

B: I lived in Mexico City.

13. Complete the conversation. Fill in the blank.

A: What _____ you going to do tomorrow?

B: I'm going to a movie.

14. Complete the conversation. Fill in the blank.

A: Were you here yesterday?

B: No, I _____ .

15. Complete the conversation. Fill in the blank.

A: _____ do you live?

B: I live in Miami.

16. Complete the sentence. Fill in the blank.

What _____ you doing when you saw the accident?

17. Complete the conversation. Fill in the blank.

A: _____ you ever worked in a bank before?

B: No, I used to work as a cashier, but that was in a restaurant.

18. Complete the conversation. Fill in the blank.

A: When _____ you talk to the boss about this matter?

B: Only yesterday.

19. Complete the conversation. Fill in the blank.

A: This letter says I've won a million dollars, but I have to buy some magazines to get the money. Do you think I should do that?

B: No, you _____ .

20. Complete the sentence. Fill in the blank.

I _____ never going to understand this tax form. It's too complicated.

Part 3

To answer questions 21 and 22, read the following ad.

> ### SALE!!! SALE!!! SALE!!!
> Peaches 10 cents each
> Tomatoes 29 cents a pound
> Red apples 5 cents each

21. You want to buy four peaches. How much will you pay? Circle the correct letter.

    a. 10 cents   b. 20 cents   c. 30 cents   d. 40 cents

22. You want to buy two pounds of tomatoes. How much will you pay? Circle the correct letter.

    a. 39 cents   b. 60 cents   c. 58 cents   d. 5 cents

To answer questions 23–25, read the memo and the story after it.

MEMO

TO: All employees

FROM: Mark

RE: Vacation time

Beginning in January of next year, Bestco Inc. will shift to the following vacation schedule.

Employees with up to 1 year of service:
1 week per year

Employees with 2–4 years of service:
2 weeks per year

Employees with 5 to 10 years of service:
3 weeks per year

Employees with more than 10 years of service:
4 weeks per year

Frank Malyszko started at Bestco at the beginning of this year. His friend Juan started two years ago. Right now, Frank has three vacation days, and Juan has a week.

23. How much vacation time will Frank have next year? Circle the correct letter.

    a. He will have one week.

    b. He will have two weeks.

    c. He will have three weeks.

    d. He will have four weeks.

24. How much vacation time will Juan have next year? Circle the correct letter.

    a. He will have one week.

    b. He will have two weeks.

    c. He will have three weeks.

    d. He will have four weeks.

25. How much vacation time does an employee get after 8 years? Circle the correct letter.

    a. one week

    b. two weeks

    c. three weeks

    d. four weeks

To answer questions 26 and 27, read the following memo.

MEMO

TO: All employees

FROM: James Ross

RE: Changes in Health Plan

Please note the following:

Those employees who now have REGNA Health Care will have to switch to a new company. Employees will be able to choose between HealthPrev Company, Keystone Health Maintenance, and Arbco Health. Here are the costs for each of these plans:

HealthPrev Company	Family Plan:	$205.00/month for a family with children
	Joint Plan:	$140.00/month for a couple without children
	Single Plan:	$105.00/month for a single employee
Keystone Health	Family Plan:	$180.00/month for a family with children
	Joint Plan:	$150.00/month for a couple without children
	Single Plan:	$90.00/month for a single employee
Arbco Health	Family Plan:	$200.00/month for a family with children
	Joint Plan:	$160.00/month for a couple without children
	Single Plan:	$80.00/month for a single employee

Employees who currently have the REGNA plan may wish to discuss it with other employees who already have one of the other three plans above.

26. Which of the plans is the cheapest for a single employee? Circle the correct letter.

     a. Keystone Health

     b. HealthPrev Company

     c. Arbco Health

     d. They are all the same.

27. Which of the plans is the most expensive for a family with children? Circle the correct letter.

     a. Keystone Health

     b. HealthPrev Company

     c. Arbco Health

     d. They are all the same.

To answer questions 28–30, read the following passage.

What do you need to do to stay healthy? Well, diet and exercise play an important role, but an important factor is avoiding things that can hurt your health. For example, if you smoke cigarettes, you have a much greater risk of heart disease and cancer than nonsmokers. Alcohol can also increase your risk for these health problems if you have several drinks each day, for example, and it can lead to liver problems also. Doctors are unsure about the risk of having only one drink a day. Drinking coffee presents some of the same risks as smoking, but smoking is worse for you. Doctors caution us to keep our consumption of caffeine low, but many Americans drink three or four cups of coffee a day, or more.

28. Which of the following health problems is not mentioned in the passage above?

    a. heart disease

    b. cancer

    c. diabetes

    d. liver problems

29. What are the health risks of having one drink a day?

    a. very serious

    b. heart disease

    c. unclear

    d. no risk at all

30. If "many Americans drink three or four cups of coffee a day, or more," which of the following is probably true?

    a. This is more of a problem than smoking cigarettes.

    b. This is not a problem for people who don't smoke.

    c. This is more than doctors think they should drink.

    d. There are no serious health risks in drinking coffee.

UNIT 1   LOOKING FOR THE RIGHT JOB

OVERVIEW

Objectives

Skills and Structures

Understand conversations about networking and getting references

Read and write a résumé

Do a career interest inventory

Understand a time line

Read and write a cover letter

Think of possible interview questions

Use present perfect tense

Use present perfect continuous tense

SCANS Competencies

Acquire and evaluate information: Student Book, Sound Bites, page 2; Student Book, Sound Bites, page 7; Student Book, Reading for Real, page 5.

Identify human resources: Student Book, Reading for Real, page 5; Workbook, Read, Think, and Write, page 5

Understand systems: Student Book, Get Graphic, page 10

Realia

Want ads, job announcements, and flyers from employment agencies

Possible visit by a job counselor

Sample cover letters

ACTIVITY NOTES

Scene 1

Refer to the general instructions on page xii in the Introduction.

Preparation

1. Introduce the topic of the unit by asking students about looking for a good job.

   • Why is it important to find a job that is right for you?

   • What good and bad job experiences have you had?

2. Photocopy a 3-column chart with these headings: *Employed, looking for a better job, Unemployed and looking for a job, Unemployed and not looking for a job*. Distribute the photocopies and have learners move around the room asking others what their situation is. Sample questions could include, "Do you have a job? Are you looking for a job?" Have learners get into the corresponding groups and discuss their reasons for being in that particular group. Have each group share reasons or situations with the class.

   Make a T-chart on an overhead transparency or on the board with these headings: *Things I want in a job, Things I don't want in a job*. Have the class brainstorm ideas and fill in the chart. Possible answers include benefits, long hours, good salary, flexible hours, or little overtime.

Presentation

1. Ask students where the people in Scene 1 are.
2. Have pairs of students read the directions and text above the comic strip.
3. Have students read the comic strip. With the class discuss any words students do not understand. Ask volunteers to explain word meanings.
4. Have students read the questions below the comic strip. Make sure students understand the questions.
5. Tell students to listen carefully as you play the tape of Scene 1.
6. Have students work in pairs or small groups to answer the questions below the comic strips, either orally or in writing. If necessary, replay the tape of Scene 1.
7. Call on students to share their answers with the class.
8. Have students retell the story of Scene 1. Ask individuals to retell it orally to the class, or to read the story from their notebook to the class.

Extension

1. Have students role-play the Scene in one of several ways. You may want to videotape students' presentations to the class so they can view them later.

Option 1: Have students perform the lines as written. You can assign partners or let students choose their own.

Option 2: Have students substitute their own job and job history for Pemba's. (They can make them up if they don't have any work experience.)

Option 3: More advanced students can continue the dialogue by either describing how to get a union card, or creating another problem and explaining how to overcome it.

2. Have students write letters to an American friend or neighbor. In the letters, have them compare the job market in the United States with the job market in their native countries using the ideas they had from the questions below the comic strips.

Page 2

Vocabulary Prompts
Refer to the general instructions on page xiv in the Introduction.

Preparation

Have students brainstorm a list of different types of jobs such as internships, apprenticeships, volunteer work, and paid work. Continue by having them come up with ideas about different ways to get a job. Write their ideas on an overhead transparency or the board.

Presentation

1. Have students work in pairs or small groups to discuss the Vocabulary Prompts.
2. Check their understanding by reading each description or definition below and have them call out or write the vocabulary item it describes.
   - Lisa worked with Patty before. Patty asks Lisa if a new employer can call and talk to her about their work experience together. (reference)
   - a possible job (job lead)
   - learning a new job by watching experienced workers and working with them (apprenticeship)

- talking to family, friends, and others about looking for a job (networking)
- things that are necessary (requirements)

3. Ask the following questions and have students give examples:
   - Has anyone ever networked?
   - Has anyone been an apprentice?
   - Has anyone given an employer references?

Sound Bites

Refer to the general instructions on page xiii in the Introduction.

Before You Listen

Preparation

1. Write the following words on the board: *union, GED, application fee, plumber, residential, position,* and *requirement.* Have students copy them into their notebooks. Make sure they understand that they will hear these words in the exercise. Ask the class if they know what these words mean. Clarify if necessary and add any related words for each item; for example, for *application fee* you may wish to add *apply* and *applicant.* Have them write the definitions or translations in their notebooks along with the part of speech for each word for future reference.

2. Read the first line under the Sound Bites heading, or have the students read it silently. Tell students to read about the three calls they are going to listen to. Make sure they read about the specific details asked for in each call.

While You Listen

Presentation

1. Tell students they will hear three phone conversations about getting a job. Explain that you will play the tape three times and that students should listen for specific details asked about each call. Tell them they do not have to write anything the first time they listen; they will write their answers when you play the tape a second time. When you play the tape a third time, students should check their answers.

2. Play the tape three times. When you play the tape the second time, have students write the information on the lines. When you play the tape the third time, students should check their answers individually.

After You Listen

Presentation

1. Have students work in pairs to compare their answers. Circulate among the students and answer any questions they may have.

2. Go over the correct answers with the class.

3. If necessary, play the tape a fourth time to clarify any parts that students may have found difficult.

Listening Script

1. **Woman:** Local 134, Electricians' Union. May I help you?

   Pemba: Yes, I'm calling about a union card. How can I get one?

   Woman: Have you enrolled in our apprenticeship program?

   Pemba: No, I haven't. What is it, exactly?

   Woman: You work and study at the same time.

   Pemba: I see . . . What do I need to do to apply?

   Woman: You need to have a high school diploma or a GED. And there's also a twenty dollar application fee.

   Pemba: Twenty dollars? OK. Thanks for the information.

   Woman: You're welcome. Thanks for calling Local 134.

2. **Nambi:** Hello?

   Pemba: Hi! It's Pemba.

   Nambi: Pemba! How are you doing?

   Pemba: Pretty good. I made a new friend. Her name's Susan.

   Nambi: Tell me more!

   Pemba: Later! Listen—You work in construction. Is anyone looking for an electrician?

   Nambi: I thought you were working at the factory.

   Pemba: Well, I've decided to do what I *really* want.

   Nambi: Hmmm. You know, there might be a possible job at that new construction company—they're hiring plumbers, electricians, everything. Have you applied there yet?

   Pemba: No, I haven't. What's the name of the company?

   Nambi: Century . . . Construction. I think that's it.

   Pemba: Century. Do you know who to call there?

   Nambi: Jay. The guy's name is Jay.

   Pemba: That's great. Hey, can I give them your name—as a reference?

   Nambi: Sure. No problem. I'm usually home after 8:00 P.M. Good luck!

3. **Jay:** Jay Neilson.

   Pemba: Hello. My name is Pemba Ibo. I understand you have an opening for an electrician?

   Jay: Yes, right now we're looking for an assistant electrician.

   Pemba: Well, I'm interested in the position.

   Jay: Can you tell me about yourself?

   Pemba: Yes. I have worked as an electrician before. I'm very hard-working, and I . . .

Jay:	Have you done any residential work?
Pemba:	You mean in homes? Yes, I have.
Jay:	Good, because that's the most important requirement. That's where we get most of our business. Well, can you come in to talk to us, say, next Wednesday the 8th? About 10:00?
Pemba:	November 8th at 10:00? Sure.
Jay:	OK. Send us a résumé, and we'll see you next week—Pemba?
Pemba:	Yes, that's right. See you next week.

Answers to Sound Bites

1. enroll in apprenticeship program; high school diploma or GED and $20 fee

2. at a new construction company; Century Construction; Jay; 8:00 P.M.

3. assistant electrician; residential work experience; Wednesday, Nov. 8, 10:00

In Your Experience

Refer to the general instructions on page xiv in the Introduction.

Preparation

Tell the class the story of how you got your job. Include other anecdotes from your job-search experience.

Presentation

1. On the board make a three-column chart with the following headings: *Friends, Newspapers,* and *Going Directly to Businesses.* Ask students to copy these headings into their notebooks.

2. Have students read the explanation about the class survey.

3. In groups of four or five, have students ask each other how they have gotten jobs in the past. Have them write each other's names under the appropriate heading in their notebooks.

4. Ask the groups to share the information they have gathered with the class. Write the information on the board under the appropriate heading.

Extension

With the class or in groups, use the information from the class survey to create a bar graph to illustrate the results.

Page 3

Spotlight on Present Perfect

Refer to the general instructions on page xv in the Introduction.

Preparation

1. Introduce the idea of the present perfect and work experience by talking about yourself. For example, you could say, "I've done a lot of different kinds of jobs in my life. I've been a babysitter. I've been a waitress. I've done housekeeping. I've sold shoes before. I've scooped ice cream. I've also taught English!"

2. Ask some students what jobs they have done. Don't make grammatical corrections at this stage. This is an opportunity to informally observe if they can produce the present perfect.

3. Make a multiple-column chart on the board. Have the class select some work settings such as factory, restaurant, hospital, or home. Write these in the column headings. Ask, for example, "How many of us have worked in a factory?" Tally the results and summarize them for the class. For example, say, "Six people have worked in a factory."

Presentation

1. Have students read about the present perfect in the Spotlight Box. Direct students' attention to the examples. Make sure they understand that the first column contains affirmative statements, the second column contains negative statements, and the third column contains yes/no questions.

2. Make sure students understand that the present perfect is formed with a form of *have* and a past participle. Focus their attention on the examples at the bottom of the box that show regular and irregular verb participles. Explain that regular verb participles are the same form as the regular past tense. Irregular verb participles will have to be memorized.

3. Ask students to say what the contractions mean (pronoun plus *have*).

4. Focus the students' attention on the placement of *not, ever,* and *never.* Elicit or point out that these words come between *have* and the participle.

Exercise 1

Refer to the general instructions on page xvi in the Introduction.

Preparation

Write several different kinds of jobs on the board. With the class brainstorm a list of possible tasks associated with each job.

Presentation

1. Have the students read the directions to the exercise. Make sure everyone understands that they are going to walk around the class and survey their classmates. If your class is very large, you might want to do this in groups.

2. Remind students to write their classmates' names on the corresponding lines. Walk around the room to make sure that all the students are participating and completing the exercise correctly.

Answers to Exercise 1

Answers will vary.

Exercise 2

Refer to the general instructions on page xvi in the Introduction.

Presentation

Have students work in pairs to share the results of their surveys. Walk around the room to make sure that each partner has a chance to participate.

Answers to Exercise 2

Answers will vary.

In Your Experience

Refer to the general instructions on page xiv in the Introduction.

Preparation

Focus students' attention on the Spotlight Box and the verbs in Exercise 1. Write some example sentences with the present perfect on the board and try to elicit the rule on how to form it.

Presentation

1. Have learners read the directions. Then tell them to create a two-column chart. Make sure they head each column as directed.
2. Tell students to work in pairs to complete the sentences. Make sure you allow enough time for them to write complete sentences.

Extension

After the students have shared their answers with each other, tally them with the class. You may want to illustrate the results of the survey in a bar or pie graph on an overhead transparency or the board.

Workbook

Workbook page 1 may be assigned after students have completed Student Book page 3.

Page 4

Person to Person

Refer to the general instructions on page xvi in the Introduction.

Preparation

1. With the class brainstorm a list of jobs and write them across the top of an overhead transparency or the board. Have the class brainstorm different tasks associated with each job and write these ideas under each job title.
2. Talk about job interviews. What sorts of information would the students expect to be asked?

   Apply those ideas to the jobs in the list. Have the class make up possible questions an interviewer might ask for those jobs.

Presentation

1. Have students read the directions. Make sure they understand what to do. Then have them read the conversation description before each conversation.
2. Read the conversations aloud. You may want to have the students repeat each line after you.
3. Have the students work with partners to finish the last conversation. Encourage them to write as many additional questions as they can. Walk around the room and make sure students are using the present perfect in their questions.
4. Have pairs practice saying the conversations. Then have each pair present the last conversation to the class, including their own questions.
5. After students practice the conversations, ask the following questions and discuss them with the class:
   - Did Pemba give good answers to each question?
   - Can you think of other answers, or better answers, he could give?

Extension

Have students discuss the additional questions for Conversation 4 that the partners created.

- Which questions create a good impression with the interviewer?
- Which questions could create a negative impression with the interviewer?
- Which questions are the most likely to come up in an interview situation?

 Option 1: Work with the class to discuss the possible ending questions to Conversation 4. Write them on the board or on an overhead transparency. Circle the best questions.

Option 2: After the class has discussed all the possible questions to end Conversation 4, group more advanced students with less advanced students to discuss which questions are the best and why. Then have each group share its opinions with the class.

Option 3: After the class has discussed all the possible questions to end Conversation 4, have students work in groups to discuss which answers are best, most probable, and what would happen if inappropriate questions were asked. Have groups share their answers with the class.

Answers to Person to Person

Answers will vary. Possible answers include the following:

When do you expect to fill the position?

What is the salary?

What will the hours be?

Your Turn

Refer to the general instructions on page xiv in the Introduction.

Preparation

Review the list of different jobs used in the Person to Person activity with the class. Focus students' attention on the tasks associated with each job.

Presentation

1. In pairs have the students choose a job from the list in the Preparation activity or another of their choosing.
2. Have them write a conversation about that job, using the conversations in Person to Person as a model.
3. Have students practice their conversations and present them to the class. You may want to encourage students to bring in props to enhance their presentations.

Page 5

Vocabulary Prompts

Refer to the general instructions on page xiv in the Introduction.

Preparation

Have learners explain and identify the words they already know.

Presentation

1. Explain any new words and phrases. Check understanding by reading each description or definition below. Have students call out or write the vocabulary item it describes.

   - my skills and background (qualifications)
   - the job I want (objective)
   - I can give you the names of people I have worked with. (references available upon request)
   - You can always count on me. (reliable)

Extension

For those learners who haven't worked before, discuss life experiences that people can use to write a résumé and find a job. For example, how can experiences such as raising children, organizing a household, helping in a family business, or volunteering demonstrate valuable work skills? Brainstorm a list of ideas.

Reading for Real

Refer to the general instructions on page xvi in the Introduction.

Preparation

Pass around sample résumés for students to examine. Ask questions such as the following:

   - Has anyone ever written a résumé before?
   - What types of information are on résumés?
   - Is the language used in the résumé formal or informal? (formal)
   - How is the information organized? Why do you think this organization is effective?

Presentation

1. Have the students read the directions and the résumé.
2. Have students scan the résumé to get information to answer the questions.
3. Check the answers with the class.

Answers to Reading for Real

1. electrician
2. reliable and hard-working
3. Answers may vary. Possible answers include the following:

   It shows that he got a promotion.

   It shows that he has good work experience in the United States. He will be able to provide good references.

Your Turn

Refer to the general instructions on page xiv in the Introduction.

Preparation

If you haven't completed the Extension activity from the Vocabulary Prompts, do so now. If you have completed it, review the ideas with the class.

Presentation

1. Have students read the directions.

2. In pairs have students help each other to write their own résumés. Walk around the room and help individuals that may be having difficulty recalling information about their job experience. Ask questions such as the following:

   - What exactly did you do? What else?

   - Did you get a promotion?

   - Is there any unpaid experience you have that would show you're a responsible, capable worker?

3. After the pairs have checked each other's work. have each pair exchange their résumés with another pair for additional feedback. Encourage the students to focus on content, spelling and grammar.

Culture Corner

Refer to the general instructions on page xvii in the Introduction.

Preparation

Ask learners the following questions:

- How are jobs changing?

- Have there been any changes in your workplace?

- In general, are jobs getting easier or more difficult to do?

Presentation

1. Have students read the directions and complete the questionnaire individually.

2. In small groups have students read the questions at the bottom of the page and discuss the results of their surveys. Walk around the class and encourage students to give reasons for their answers.

3. Discuss the results of the survey. For the sometimes and never answers, have the class discuss which solutions seem best. If there are some questions that students have not found a solution to, have the class brainstorm possibilities.

Extension

With the class tally the results of the questionnaire to find out the strengths and weaknesses of the people in the class. The students can use this information to help each other consider different job possibilities. For example, if several people like to solve problems, what kinds of jobs are best suited for this strength? Who has such a job? Are there any openings where this person works?

Scene 2

Refer to the general instructions on page xviii in the Introduction.

Preparation

Quickly review the story line from Scene 1: Pemba has just met Susan at a party. He tells her that he's working in a factory now, but back in Nigeria he was an electrician. He seems unhappy. He doesn't have a union card to work as an electrician, and he doesn't know how to get one.

Presentation

1. Ask students where the people in Scene 2 are.

2. Have pairs of students read the directions and text above the comic strip.

3. Have students read the comic strip. With the class discuss any words students do not understand. Ask volunteers to explain word meanings.

4. Have students read the questions below the comic strip. Make sure students understand the questions.

5. Tell students to listen carefully as you play the tape of Scene 2.

6. Have students work in pairs or small groups to answer the questions below the comic strips, either orally or in writing. If necessary, replay the tape of Scene 2.

7. Call on students to share their answers with the class.

8. Have students retell the story of Scene 2. Ask individuals to retell it orally, or to read the story from their notebook, to the class.

Extension

Have students role-play the Scene in one of several ways. You may want to video-tape students' presentations to the class so they can view them later.

 Option 1: Have students perform the lines as written. You can assign partners or let students choose their own.

Option 2: Have students substitute other job-search techniques in the dialogue. They can refer to Student Book page 2 for ideas.

Option 3: More advanced students can continue the dialogue by having the job counselor suggest other job-search techniques.

Vocabulary Prompts

Refer to the general instructions on page xiv in the Introduction.

Preparation

Have students identify and explain words they already know.

Presentation

1. Have students work in groups to talk about the new words.

2. Check comprehension by reading each description or definition below. Have students call out or write the vocabulary item it describes:

   - evaluation of a person's performance at a job (reviews)
   - important thing to think about (concern)
   - place where you can buy things less expensively from a company (outlet store)
   - possible people for a job (candidates)

Sound Bites

Refer to the general instructions on page xiii in the Introduction.

Preparation

1. Refer students to the comic strip in Scene 2. Tell them they will hear a conversation between Pemba and the Director of Maintenance at the factory.

2. Write the following words on the board: *personnel, switching over, maintenance, retire, keep a log, We'll get back to you,* and *advance.* Have the students copy them into their notebooks. Make sure they understand that they will hear these words

and phrases in the exercise. Ask the class if they know what the words or phrases mean. Clarify if necessary and add any related words for each item. For example, along with *maintenance* you could write *maintain*. Have students write the definitions or translations in their notebooks along with the part of speech for each word for future reference.

While You Listen

Presentation

1. Have students read the directions and the questions.

2. Have students get their notebooks out to prepare for note taking.

3. Explain that you will play the tape three times and that students should listen for information to answer the questions Tell them they do not have to write anything the first time they listen; they will write their notes when you play the tape a second time. When you play the tape a third time, students should check and add to their notes.

2. Play the tape three times. When you play the tape the second time, have students take notes in their notebooks. When you play the tape the third time, students should check that their notes answer the questions.

After You Listen

Presentation

1. In small groups have students discuss the answers to the questions. Circulate among the students and answer any questions they may have. Go over the correct answers with the class.

2. If necessary, play the tape a fourth time to clarify any parts that students may have found difficult.

Extension

1. Have students research job resources in their local community. Where can they find jobs? Make a bulletin board in the class. Post job announcements, flyers from temporary agencies, and so on.

2. If possible, have a job counselor or recruiter visit the class to discuss job-search strategies.

Listening Script

Jerry:	Hey, Pemba. Have a seat.
Pemba:	Hi, Jerry.
Jerry:	They told me in Personnel that you're interested in switching over to Maintenance?
Pemba:	Well, I'm especially interested in the electrician job—the one that was listed a few days ago?
Jerry:	Yeah, we've got someone retiring. Now I've looked at your résumé. You've only been an electrician in Nigeria?
Pemba:	That's correct, but I've been talking to some of the maintenance people about what they do, and I'm sure I could learn the job quickly.

Jerry:	And your communication skills? In this job, you'd have to talk to people and keep a log to explain what you do each day.
Pemba:	I've been taking English classes, and I feel comfortable communicating with people.
Jerry:	Uh-huh. Now this job would mean a lot of traveling around to our outlet stores.
Pemba:	That's fine with me. That's no problem.
Narrator:	*The Director asks Pemba some more specific questions and then . . .*
Jerry:	Well . . . we have a few more candidates to interview, but we should be making our decision soon. We'll get back to you.
Pemba:	Thanks, Jerry. I'm really looking forward to this opportunity—I've been working here for a year, and I'd like to stay with the company.
Jerry:	Well, your reviews have all been good. We like to see workers advance. Thanks for coming in.
Pemba:	Thanks a lot, Jerry.

Answers to Sound Bites

Answers may vary. Possible answers include the following:

1. What concerns or questions does Jerry have?

   Jerry is concerned that Pemba's experience is only in Nigeria. He's also concerned about Pemba's communication skills and the amount of travel involved.

2. What answers does Pemba give?

   Pemba says that he has talked to some of the maintenance people about their jobs and he's sure he could learn the job quickly. He also says that he's been taking English classes and feels comfortable communicating with people. He has no problem with the amount of travel.

3. Does Pemba get the job?

   Pemba does not get the job on the spot but is told that a decision should be made soon. He'll be notified.

Page 8

Spotlight on Present Perfect Continuous with *For* and *Since*

Refer to the general instructions on page xv in the Introduction.

Preparation

1. Introduce the concept of present perfect continuous and *for* and *since* by talking about yourself. Stress that the present perfect always relates somehow to now, the present.

   Draw a time line like the one in the Spotlight Box. Talk about your teaching experience. Write the corresponding years on the time line. Say something like the following: "I'm teaching English now. I've been teaching English for a long time. I've been teaching since 1981. I started then, and I'm still teaching now. I've been working at this school since 1990. Lately, I've been teaching the more advanced levels. I like it because advanced learners can really talk and have good discussions!"

2. Look at the attendance roster. Draw a time line, and with the class, talk about how long students have been coming to class. For example, say, "Estela has been coming to class since August. She's been studying here for four months."

Presentation

1. Have students read about present perfect continuous with *for* and *since* in the Spotlight Box.

2. Direct students' attention to the example question and answers in the Spotlight Box. Make sure they understand how the present perfect continuous is formed and what it means.

3. Make sure students understand the differences between a point in time and a period of time. Emphasize that *since* is used to talk about a starting point in time and *for* is used to talk about a period of time.

Exercise 3

Refer to the general instructions on page xvi in the Introduction.

Preparation

Lead a discussion about different things the class has been doing since it started. Write the ideas on the board . Use the exact words students say. Go over the sentences and underline the present perfect continuous forms. Discuss and correct as necessary. Do the same for *since* and *for*.

- We've been using *Contemporary English* Book 4 since the first day of class.
- We've been getting to know our classmates for (two) weeks.

Presentation

1. Have students read the directions and complete the exercise.

2. In pairs have students check their answers.

3. Explain that some words, such as *know* and *be*, cannot be used in the present perfect continuous. Can students understand why?

Answers to Exercise 3

1. since 2. have been looking 3. has been helping 4. have been living 5. for

Your Turn

Refer to the general instructions on page xiv in the Introduction.

Preparation

Ask a student to model the activity with you. Ask him or her the questions in Your Turn and write the answers on the board.

Presentation

1. Have the students read the directions. Then have them work in pairs to ask each other questions about their lives in the United States. Have them refer to the letter in Exercise 3 as an example.

2. Walk around the room and listen to the students and make sure they are using *for* and *since* in their answers.

3. Have students tell the class about their partners.

Extension

Have students write letters about their lives to a friend or family member in their native country. Use the letter in Exercise 3 and the information from Your Turn.

Workbook

Workbook page 2 may be assigned after students have completed Student Book page 8.

Page 9

Spotlight on Simple Past, Present Perfect, and Present Perfect Continuous

Refer to the general instructions on page xv in the Introduction.

Preparation

Ask students to cover the fill-in part of the exercise and focus on the calendar. For each item on Pemba's calendar, ask students to try to relate that activity to the present (for example, to December, on the calendar). Ask, "Is each activity still going on?" If so, have them use that verb in the present perfect or present perfect continuous in a sentence. Point out that one-time events such as *met Susan* and *called about a union card* are not still going on and must remain in the simple past. This will set the stage for the grammatical decisions students will need to make in the exercise.

Presentation

1. Have students read the examples illustrating the differences between the simple past, the present perfect, and the present perfect continuous in the Spotlight Box.
2. Focus students' attention on the time lines. Ask individual students to create sentences using each of these tenses.

Exercise 4

Refer to the general instructions on page xvi in the Introduction.

Preparation

Direct students' attention to Pemba's calendar. Write *February* on the board and have the class make up an event for Pemba. Then have students work in pairs to write a sentence about Pemba using the information for February and one of the tenses in the Spotlight Box. Have partners write their sentences on the board. Ask them to underline the verb form they used. With the class discuss the sentences. Ask, "Did they use the correct verb form? Did they use *for* or *since* correctly? If not, how could the sentence be rewritten to make it correct?"

Presentation

1. Have the students read the directions and complete the exercise.
2. With the class check the answers. For items where the students had difficulty, discuss why that item required that particular form. Use the time lines in the Spotlight Box to illustrate the reasons.

Extension

In pairs have students write additional events on Pemba's calendar. Have them write sentences describing each event using Exercise 4 as a model. Have the students share their sentences with the class.

Answers to Exercise 4

1. moved
2. has lived/has been living
3. has worked/has been working
4. started
5. has studied/has been studying

6. met
7. has known
8. decided
9. called
10. has decided

Your Turn

Refer to the general instructions on page xiv in the Introduction.

Preparation

Have students brainstorm a list of important events that happened to them during the past year. Encourage them to remember approximate dates for each event.

Presentation

1. Have students read the directions.
2. Have students write a letter to a friend about the events in their lives during the past year. Have them refer to their Preparation activity list for ideas and dates. They should use the letter in Exercise 3 as a model.
3. Have each student exchange letters with a partner and check to make sure that the simple past, present perfect and present perfect continuous have been used correctly. They should also check to make sure that all the ideas are clearly expressed and the spelling is accurate. Any problems should be discussed in pairs.
4. After letters have been returned and corrected, tell students to share their letters in groups or with the class.

Workbook

Workbook pages 3 and 4 may be assigned after students have completed Student Book page 9.

Page 10

Vocabulary Prompts

Refer to the general instructions on page xiv in the Introduction.

Preparation

Have students identify and explain words they already know.

Presentation

1. Have students work in groups to talk about the new words.
2. Check comprehension by reading each description or definition below. Have students call out or write the vocabulary item it describes.
   - an available job (job opening)
   - a notice about an available job in a newspaper (want ad)
   - people who are trying for the same thing (competition)
   - graph that looks like a pie (pie graph)

Get Graphic

Refer to the general instructions on page xviii in the Introduction.

Preparation

1. If students are unfamiliar with pie graphs, explain that they provide a visual way to compare a part of something to the whole.

2. Conduct a poll before looking at the graph. Ask, "How do people find jobs in the U.S.?" Brainstorm a list of ways to find jobs (for example, *read the newspaper*) With the class, assign percentages of use to each strategy.

3. Make an overhead transparency of the pie graph or draw it on the board. Point to the different sections. Then compare the hypotheses the class made with the information in the pie graph. Were their hypotheses correct?

Presentation

Have students study the pie chart and read the different stages of the hidden job market.

Check comprehension by reading the following statements aloud and having students call out the stage each one represents.

- "They just announced a job opening in the mailroom. It hasn't been put in the newspaper yet. Hurry and apply!" (Stage 3)

- "We don't have any positions now, but you seem to have a lot of good experience. Do you have a copy of your résumé?" (Stage 1)

- "I'm calling about the assembler's position I saw in the Classifieds. Is the job still available?" (Stage 4)

- "They said in the meeting that they definitely need another mechanic on second shift. Why don't you talk to Larry and say you're interested?" (Stage 2)

Exercise 5

Refer to the general instructions on page xvi in the Introduction.

Preparation

On the board write the following statement. "By the end of Stage 3, 65% of all possible jobs are filled." Have students scan the time line to find the information that will prove the statement true or false. With the class review the answer (the answer is false). Ask students to show the class where they found the information.

Presentation

1. Have students read the directions and work in small groups to complete the exercise. Tell them to refer to the pie chart and the time line.

2. Circulate among students and answer any questions they might have.

3. Go over the answers with the class. If there are any discrepancies have students refer to specific information in the time line or the pie chart to support their answers.

Answers to Exercise 5

1. false   2. true   3. false   4. false   5. true   6. false

In Your Experience

Refer to the general instructions on page xiv in the Introduction.

Preparation

Lead a discussion about job-search techniques students have used in the past. Have them refer to their ideas from the In Your Experience activity on page 2.

Presentation

1. Have students read the directions and discuss their opinions. Then share ideas with the class.

2. Ask students if they have ever used one of the methods listed to get a job. Was it successful? Have them share their experiences with the class.

Activity Masters

Activity Master 1-1 can be introduced any time after Student Book page 10 has been completed.

Preparation

1. Write a list of professions on the board. Be sure to use a wide variety and salary range. Have students speculate on the kind of education required for each profession.

2. Have students make guesses about the annual salary for each profession.

Presentation

1. Have students study the information in the chart. Then have them read the directions and each statement. Students should decide individually whether each statement is true or false according to the information in the chart.

2. In pairs have students check their answers.

Page 11

Issues and Answers

Refer to the general instructions on page xix in the Introduction.

Presentation

Have students read the cover letter individually. Remind them that they can refer to Pemba's résumé on page 5 if necessary.

Your Turn

Refer to the general instructions on page xiv in the Introduction.

Preparation

1. Collect sample cover letters from friends, your own files, or other sources. Have students familiarize themselves with the different parts of a cover letter (date, heading, greeting, body, closing). Cut up some letters and have students sequence the different sections. Have students evaluate which letters are better than others and why.

2. Bring in several copies of the Classified section of the local newspaper and copies of various job listings from companies. Ask students the following questions:

   - What exactly is this employer looking for?

   - How can I show that I'm uniquely qualified for the position?

3. After students have written cover letters to go with the résumés they wrote on page 5, have them work in pairs to read and make corrections as indicated.

4. Choose a few letters to copy on a transparency to share with the class. Encourage the class to comment on their strengths and suggest ways the letters could be improved.

5. Have students collectively draft a letter on the board for a real classmate applying for a real job from the ads and listings you brought in. Make sure students understand that résumés and cover letters are just one part of the "packaging" in getting a job. When going for an interview, your appearance and the impression you make in person can be more influential than the cover letter and résumé.

Presentation

1. Have students read the directions and the model cover letter. Then have them write a cover letter to go with their résumés. They should refer to the cover letter in Issues and Answers for another example.

2. Have students exchange their letters with a partner. The partner should check to make sure that the letter is organized correctly, the ideas are clearly stated, and the grammar and spelling are accurate. They should discuss any problem areas with their partners and help each other find solutions.

 Option 1: Have less advanced students write a list of things that have been happening in their lives instead of writing a cover letter.

Option 2: Have more advanced students write additional paragraphs after they have finished their cover letters. These paragraphs can describe how they got jobs in their native country, what that work experience was like, and what additional work experiences they have that will help them get their next jobs.

Page 12

Wrap-Up

Refer to the general instructions on page xix in the Introduction.

Preparation

1. Lead a discussion about interviews by asking the following questions:
   - How should you prepare for an interview? (prepare answers to questions about your job, your work history, your strengths and weaknesses as a worker, your goals, etc.)
   - How should you dress for an interview (professionally)
   - Is it important to be on time for an interview? (yes)
   - What kinds of questions do you think a person might be asked in an interview (Answers will vary. Write students' ideas on the board.)

2. Have students share any interview experience they have had with the class. Ask, "What kinds of questions were you asked? How did you answer? Did you get the job?"

Presentation

1. Have students read the directions and work in small groups to fill out the chart.

2. Ask groups to share their possible questions and answers with each other.

3. Have students choose a job from the want ads or any other source they want. In pairs students should interview each other for the jobs they want, using the questions and answers from the chart.

4. After the interview have students critique the performances of the candidates, using the questions in Wrap-Up.

Extension

Save the interview questions each group produces and put them on index cards. Use them for review, as a basis for videotaped mock interviews, or for a two-team competition (with a "judge" or panel to assign points earned).

Think About Learning

Refer to the general instructions on page xix in the Introduction.

Preparation

Explain to students that they can think about their learning in each unit of the book. In this way they can monitor how much progress they make and the areas in which they think they need to do better. Students will thus have greater control over what they learn and will be able to give better feedback to the teacher about what is difficult and what is easy for them. Encourage students to fill in their charts and provide feedback about how they think they are doing.

Presentation

1. Tell students to fill in their charts individually.

2. Explain that they can look up the pages where they worked on a specific skill or structure. The page references are provided in the second column of the chart.

3. Circulate among students to answer any questions they might have.

4. Encourage students to add extra details in the bottom row of the chart. If they do not wish to comment on something else they have learned, they can make comments about what they would like to do.

5. Encourage students to share their feedback with you. Make it clear to them that they will not be graded on this self-assessment.

Workbook

Workbook pages 5 and 6 may be assigned after students have completed Student Book page 12.

Activity Masters

Activity Master 1-2 can be assigned after page 12 has been completed.

Preparation

Ask students if they have ever seen the television game show *Jeopardy*. Ask individuals to explain how the game works.

Presentation

1. Divide the class into teams A and B. Cut out the headings and the ten "point" squares and tape them to the blackboard as shown below.

Content						Grammar				
10	20	30	40	50		10	20	30	40	50

2. Team A begins by having an individual team member chose a category and level of difficulty—for example, *Grammar for 30 points.*

3. The teacher reads a question according to the grid. If the question is answered correctly, Team A gets the 30 points. If it is not correct, a member of Team B can attempt to answer. The same question can keep going from team to team, but different individuals must respond each time. The team with the most points wins.

4. You may decide whether teammates can help one another. You may want to make the rule that if one team calls out the answer, points can be awarded to the opposite team.

ANSWERS TO PROGRESS CHECKS

Progress Check A

Speak or Write

Answers will vary. Here are some possible answers.

1. He's working as an assembler now, and he's done some other factory jobs.

2. No, he doesn't seem happy. He needs a union card to work as an electrician again.

3. He wants help finding a job.

Listening Script

What skills will you need for the jobs of the future? Many kinds of skills. You will need to organize time, money, and materials. You will need to work as a team with others who may be very different from you. You will need to get information, understand it, and communicate it to others. You will need to understand how systems work and how to make them better. You will need to use technology. Jobs are becoming more complex. If you are willing to learn, however, you will be ready for the jobs that lie ahead.

Listen

1. No   2. Yes   3. Yes   4. No   5. Yes

Progress Check B

Language Structures

1. moved
2. has lived/has been living
3. worked
4. got
5. has worked/has been working
6. became

Content

A. 1. c   2. a   3. d   4. b

B. 1. false   2. false

ANSWERS TO ACTIVITY MASTERS

Activity Master 1-1

1. true   2. true   3. false   4. true

Activity Master 1-2

Content

10 pts. résumé

20 pts. talking to family, friends, past co-workers, and others to find a job

30 pts. false

40 pts. false

50 pts. talking to people and going directly to companies

Grammar

10 pts. present perfect

20 pts. Answers will vary.

30 pts. worked, haven't or have never

40 pts. Tom has been working here since 1992.

50 pts. Jose and Maria have been living here for _____ years. (Answers will vary.)

UNIT 1

WORKBOOK ANSWERS

Practice 1
1. have worked   2. Have, worked   3. haven't
4. have, got   5. have done

Practice 2
1. The cook has been working in this restaurant for five years.

2. Francisco has been sending out résumés for two months.

3. Tom and Elida have been in the housekeeping department since May.

Practice 3
1. John graduated from college in 1993.

2. He has worked for Will Electronics Company since 1995.

3. He has been a supervisor since 1995.

4. Answers may vary. Here are some possible answers.
   He completed Cal-Technics training between 1991 and 1993.
   He completed the training by 1993.

Name _____ Date _____

UNIT 1   PROGRESS CHECK A

SPEAK OR WRITE

Look at the pictures from Unit 1. Use the questions below to talk or write about each picture. Retell the story in your own words.

Questions

1. Tell about Pemba's job search situation.

2. Is Pemba happy? Why or why not? Explain.

3. Why is he talking to the job counselor?

LISTEN

While you listen, put a check (✓) under *Yes* or *No*.

	Yes	No
1. This is an ad for a job opening.	_____	_____
2. Jobs are getting more complex.	_____	_____
3. Working with others is important.	_____	_____
4. Technology may not be needed.	_____	_____
5. Being a good learner can help.	_____	_____

UNIT 1   PROGRESS CHECK B

LANGUAGE STRUCTURES

Look at Sergei's time line. Write the correct tense in the story. Use simple past, present perfect, or present perfect continuous. Sometimes there may be several correct answers.

Sergei's time line				
1993	**1994**	**1995**	**1996**	**1998** (now)
moved to the U.S.	started working as a busboy	started studying English	started working in print shop	became assistant manager of print shop

Sergei (1) *move* _____ to the United States in 1993. It is now 1998. Sergei (2) *live* _____ in the United States for five years now. First he (3) *work* _____ as a busboy for a year. Then after studying some English, he (4) *get* _____ a better job in a print shop. He (5) *work* _____ there for two years now, and just last week he (6) *become* _____ an assistant manager. He is happy now.

CONTENT

A. Match Column A with Column B.

Column A		**Column B**
1. network	_____	a. the job you want
2. objective	_____	b. studies and works
3. reference	_____	c. talk to friends, others
4. apprentice	_____	d. person to talk about your past work

B. True or False?

1. The "hidden job market" means the newspaper. _____

2. It is better to write to employers than to go to people or companies directly. _____

REPRODUCIBLE MASTER
UNIT 1 ACTIVITY MASTER 1-1

MORE GRAPHIC SKILLS

Look at the chart about the jobs outlook.

JOB OUTLOOK FOR THE LATE 1990s

**Work experience plus bachelor's degree or higher
(Entry-level positions)**

Accountants	$25,000–$42,000
Marketing managers	$30,000–$54,000
Lawyers	$59,000–$88,000

Bachelor's degree

Teachers, elementary	$33,000–$40,000

Associate's degree

Registered nurses	$32,000–$44,000
Police officers	$32,000–$38,000

Vocational training

Secretaries	$17,000–$28,000
Cooks	$14,000–$29,000
Auto mechanics	$23,000–$35,000
Licensed practical nurses	$21,000–$27,000

Answer the questions. Check *True* or *False*.

	True	**False**
1. Work experience plus a bachelor's degree can earn you the highest salary of those listed above.	_____	_____
2. Some people with associate's degrees can earn more than people with bachelor's degrees.	_____	_____
3. Registered nurses earn less than licensed practical nurses.	_____	_____
4. Starting salaries for secretaries are lower than starting salaries for auto mechanics.	_____	_____

ACTIVITY MASTER 1-2

Note: See Teacher's Manual page 20 for complete directions on this activity.

✂

Content

| 10 | 20 | 30 | 40 | 50 |

Grammar

| 10 | 20 | 30 | 40 | 50 |

✂

Content

10 A one-page summary of your qualifications is called a _____

20 What is networking?

30 True or false? In an interview, employers can ask if you are married if they explain the reason for the question.

40 True or false? Reading and writing will no longer be necessary for most jobs of the future.

50 According to Unit 1, what are the two ways most people found jobs in the U.S.?.

Grammar

"I have worked as a landscaper" is an example of what?

Talk about your job experience. Use the present perfect.

Finish this sentence: "I have _____ in a restaurant, but I used a cash register."

Use the present perfect continuous:
Tom started working here in 1997. He's still here.

Use the present perfect continuous and *for*:
Jose and Maria moved here in 1995. They're still living here.

UNIT 2

TRANSPORTATION UPS AND DOWNS

OVERVIEW

Objectives

Skills and Structures

Talk about travel

Understand travel announcements

Read an employee manual

Talk about things we do in our cars, such as eat or bank

Understand a conversation with an insurance agent

Read about air fares

Read and solve problems

Use a window to organize ideas

Use reported speech

Use the present perfect

Use the past perfect

SCANS Competencies

Interpret and communicate information: Student Book, Reading for Real, page 17

Think creatively: Student Book, Culture Corner, page 18

Do problem solving: Student Book, Issues and Answers, page 23

Realia

An accident report

A newspaper police report

Bus or train maps

State or regional maps

Advice columns

ACTIVITY NOTES

Page 13

Scene 1

Refer to the general instructions on page xii in the Introduction.

Preparation

1. Introduce the topic of the unit by discussing the meaning of the unit's title. Make sure the students understand that ups and downs means good experiences and bad.

2. Make a class list of as many types of transportation as learners can think of. Do a class survey to find out how many learners have used each type of transportation. If there is time, use the information from the class survey to make a chart for additional reading or discussion practice.

3. Encourage learners to share any unusual transportation-related experiences they might have had.

Vocabulary Prompts

Refer to the general instructions on page xiv in the Introduction.

Presentation

After the students discuss the Vocabulary Prompts in small groups, ask for definitions or examples of the words. Explain any words the students do not know.

Sound Bites

Refer to the general instructions on page xiii in the Introduction.

Preparation

1. Refer to the class list of different modes of transportation. What people work with each mode?

2. Ask students to give examples of different things they might hear from someone working on a bus, a plane, a ferry, or a courtesy van.

While You Listen

Preparation

1. Make sure the students know the meanings of *flight attendant, board, ferry, steward,* and *waiting lounge.* Explain that a courtesy van is one that is free. It is offered by some hotels and companies to the airport or to homes, etc.

2. Have the students focus on the pictures and what kind of transportation is being depicted in each.

3. Read the first line under the Sound Bites heading or have students read it silently.

Presentation

1. Have the students read the directions. Make sure they understand that they will be filling in a chart with information they hear and that they can circle more than one answer.

2. Tell the students you will be playing the tape three times. The first time they should just listen for important information. The second time they hear the tape, students should fill in the chart with the information they hear. You may want to stop the tape between speakers to allow the students time to write their answers. The third time the students hear the tape, they should check their answers individually.

After You Listen

Presentation

1. Have the students work in small groups to make sentences about the travel announcements.

2. After the groups share their answers with another group, have them share their answers with the rest of the class.

Extension

1. Divide learners into pairs or groups. Play the tape or read the announcements again. Ask each pair or group to write one question about each announcement. Have the learners give their questions to another pair or group. Play the tape or read the announcements again and have learners answer the questions.

2. Divide learners into groups of three. Ask each group to write a transportation announcement.

 Option 1: Have each person in the group write one pre-listening question and one post-listening question. Have the groups get together and ask each other their questions. Compare questions and answers as a class.

Option 2: Have one person in the group write one or two pre-listening questions. Have another person read the announcement. Have the third person ask the class post-listening questions.

Option 3: For more advanced students have the groups tape record their announcements and questions.

Listening Script

1. This is your flight attendant. Our flight 664 from Miami has just landed at Chicago O'Hare International Airport. The pilot is waiting for clearance to proceed to the gate. We will deplane in approximately ten minutes at Gate B 6. Please remain seated until after the pilot has turned off the Fasten Seat Belt sign.

2. This is your bus driver with the final boarding call for all passengers leaving on Bus 72 for Normal, Illinois, and Indianapolis, Indiana. Please move to the back of the bus and sit in the first empty seat you find. If you cannot fit your carry-ons under the seat in front of you, please give them to me before you board the bus.

3. Attention all passengers for the Star of the Sea Ferry. This is your captain. The ferry will be leaving in five minutes for Port Charles. Please have your tickets ready to show to the stewards.

4. This is Ted, the courtesy van driver. Customers needing rides from Anderson Autos to their homes should leave the waiting lounge immediately. The courtesy van is located outside the service area. Exit through the door marked Cashier. There is no fee for this service.

Answers to Sound Bites

1. Chicago O'Hare International; b
2. Normal, Illinois; b, c
3. Port Charles; b
4. customer's homes; b

Your Turn

Refer to the general instructions on page xiv in the Introduction.

Preparation

Lead a discussion about public address announcements. Ask the following questions:

- Where do you usually hear announcements?
- What kind of information is given in these announcements?
- Who has heard an announcement lately? Where? What was it about?

Presentation

1. If the students can not think of an announcement they have heard recently, have them make one up. Make sure the students understand that it's not important to remember the announcement word for word and that they can paraphrase when they write it.

2. As a quick assessment ask individuals to read their announcements aloud and see if the class can guess where each came from.

Spotlight on Reported Speech

Refer to the general instructions on page xv in the Introduction.

Preparation

1. Explain that reported speech is telling what someone else said.

2. Before learners read the Spotlight Box, ask several learners the following questions:

   - How did you get to school today?

   - How long did it take?

   - What time did you arrive at school?

   On the board write the learners' answers in the three ways shown in the grammar box: direct speech, reported speech with *that,* and reported speech without *that.* Underline the verbs in the sentences and talk about how the placement of the verbs has changed. Call learners' attention to the verbs in the direct speech examples. Ask students to tell you the tense. Then call learners' attention to the verbs in the reported speech examples. Ask students to tell you the verb tenses in those sentences. Emphasize that when we use reported speech, we use a form of the past tense. If direct speech is in the present tense, reported speech is in the simple past. If direct speech uses the present continuous, reported speech uses the past continuous.

Presentation

Have students read the Spotlight Box. Make sure they understand that including *that* in reported speech is optional.

Exercise I

Refer to the general instructions on page xvi in the Introduction.

Answers to Exercise I

1. Raul said (that) he needed to get the brakes on his car fixed.

2. Emma said (that) she was late to work today because her car broke down.

3. Maria said (that) she was looking for someone to car pool with her.

4. John said (that) he liked to ride his bicycle to work on nice days.

5. Mel said (that) he wanted to buy a new car next year.

6. Luke said (that) he would be late for work tomorrow.

Your Turn

Refer to the general instructions on page xiv in the Introduction.

Presentation

As the students work in pairs, circulate around the room to make sure that everyone is using reported speech correctly.

Person to Person

Refer to the general instructions on page xvi in the Introduction.

Preparation

Make sure the students understand the difference between a minivan and a full-sized car. Explain that a long weekend is one in which you take the Friday before the weekend or the Monday after the weekend as vacation. Ask if any one has to fill out vacation request forms at work when they want to take time off from work. Ask those individuals to explain what information those forms require.

In Your Experience

Refer to the general instructions on page xiv in the Introduction.

Presentation

After learners have talked about places they have traveled to for work or vacations, make a class chart of places they have been to recently and how they got there.

Extension

Use the chart to practice writing sentences with direct and reported speech.

 Option 1: Pair more advanced students with less advanced students to write the sentences about one trip. Ask for volunteers to write their sentences on the board.

Option 2: Have the students work in pairs. Then ask one person to say where they recently traveled to, and the other person use reported speech to tell the class.

Option 3: Instead of using single events, have the students work in pairs to talk about many different traveling experiences. Then have the partners tell the class about all of their partner's experiences.

Workbook

Workbook pages 7 and 8 can be assigned after students have completed Student Book page 16.

Vocabulary Prompts

Refer to the general instructions on page xiv in the Introduction.

Presentation

Circulate around the room to make sure the groups have the correct meanings for each word.

Reading for Real

Refer to the general instructions on page xvi in the Introduction.

Preparation

1. Lead a class discussion about vacation requests and employee manuals. Conduct the survey below and write students' responses on the board. Use the answers to make a chart.

   - Raise your hand if your company gives employees a manual about benefits.
   - Raise your hand if you have problems understanding the manual.
   - Raise your hand if your company gives employees paid vacations.
   - Raise your hand if you have taken a paid vacation in the last year.
   - Raise your hand if you had to fill out a vacation request.
   - Raise your hand if you had any problems filling out the form.

2. Ask learners to work with a partner to write three to five sentences about the information in the chart. Encourage learners to elaborate on their answers where appropriate.

Exercise 2

Refer to the general instructions on page xvi in the Introduction.

Presentation

When you check students' answers, ask them to find the information in the text that supports their answers.

Extension

After learners have read the vacation request, have them circle or underline the words in the Vocabulary Prompts box. Ask students to rewrite the sentences in which the words appear, using their own words. Ask for volunteers to write their new sentences on the board. Here is an example:

   - Vacation time is awarded according to years of service with the company.
   - Rewrite: Paid vacation time depends on how long you have worked at the company.

Answers to Exercise 2

1. b   2. c   3. c   4. b   5. b

Talk About It

Refer to the general instructions on page xvi in the Introduction.

Presentation

Have the students work in small groups to complete the activity.

Culture Corner

Refer to the general instructions on page xvii in the Introduction.

Preparation

Lead a discussion about the use of cars in the students' native countries. Ask the following questions to lead the discussion:

- Are there as many cars on the road in your country as there are in the United States?
- What is the traffic situation like in your major cities?
- What are the road conditions like? Are there large highways? Are all the roads paved?
- How do most people in your country get to work and school?
- How do most people in your country get to the market and do errands?

Presentation

1. Have the students read Culture Corner. Then have them survey each other in small groups. Have each group report back to the class.

2. Make a chart or graph to illustrate the results of the survey. Ask individuals to use reported speech when they report to the class. For example, one learner asks a group, "How many people have drivers' licenses?" Then another learner uses the answer to make a sentence with reported speech. For example, "Three people said they had drivers' licenses."

Exercise 3

Refer to the general instructions on page xvi in the Introduction.

Answers to Exercise 3

Answers will vary.

Exercise 4

Refer to the general instructions on page xvi in the Introduction.

Preparation

Tell learners you are going to read a list of drive-up businesses to them. After each number they should write *yes* or *no*. *Yes* means this is a real business. *No* means this is not a real business. (All the businesses are real according to an article in the Chicago Tribune on Thursday, April 9, 1998. If you have Internet access, print out a copy of this story.)

1. Cigar stores	2. Liquor stores	3. Candy stores
4. Funeral casket sales	5. Wedding chapels	6. Divorces
7. Church services	8. Flu shot providers	

Answers to Exercise 4

Answers will vary.

Your Turn

Refer to the general instructions on page xiv in the Introduction.

Presentation

As a variation to making a list of drive-ups and drive-throughs in their neighborhoods, have learners draw maps of their neighborhoods and present them to the class.

In Your Experience

Refer to the general instructions on page xiv in the Introduction.

Presentation

You may want to include the drive-ups and drive-throughs mentioned in the Preparation for Exercise 4.

Page 19

Scene 2

Refer to the general instructions on page xviii in the Introduction.

Preparation

Find out which students in the class have ever been in a car accident. Ask individuals to tell the story of the accident. You may want to have them draw diagrams on the board to illustrate their stories. Then lead a discussion about car accidents by asking the following questions:

- Was anyone hurt in the accident? What happened to them?
- Whose fault was the accident?
- What happened to the car? Was it repaired?
- Were insurance companies involved? Who paid the bills for the accident?
- What are the procedures when there is a car accident in your native country?

Sound Bites

Refer to the general instructions on page xiii in the Introduction.

Before You Listen

Preparation

1. Write *injured* and *insurance agent* on the board. Have students copy these words and any related words (*injury, insure*) into their notebooks. Ask the class if they know what these words mean. Clarify if necessary. Have the students write the definitions or translations in their notebooks.

2. Refer to the comic strip in Scene 2. Tell the students that they will hear a conversation between Ted and his car insurance agent.

After You Listen

Presentation

1. As students check their answers in pairs or in groups, have students answer these additional questions:

   - Where does Ted have to go? (He has to go to the police station.)
   - What does Ted have to get? (He has to get a copy of the police report.)
   - How do you think Ted feels after talking to the insurance agent? (He probably feels angry and frustrated.)
   - What do you think will happen to Ted in this situation? (Answers will vary.)

2. Have the students act out their conversations about accidents.

Option 1: Have students write six- to eight-line conversations. Then they can read aloud the lines they wrote.

Option 2: Have students write a comprehensive conversation between a driver and an insurance agent about an accident using the conversation in Sound Bites as an example. Have the students present their conversations to the class. Encourage them to draw a diagram of the accident on the board or an overhead transparency to support their conversation.

Option 3: Have the class make up an interesting car-accident story. Name the drivers and their insurance agents. Then divide the class into four groups. One group is Driver A, one group is Driver A's insurance agent, one group is Driver B, and one group is Driver B's insurance agent. Have the groups work together to write conversations between each driver and his or her insurance agent, between the drivers, and between the insurance agents. Have them include diagrams of the accident to support their stories and fill out an accident report. You may want to include another group to take the role of a police officer and have the students create conversations between the police officer and each driver. Then have the different members of each group present the various conversations.

Extension

1. Have the students compile the information they gathered about their insurance companies in Before You Listen. Write the information on the board or have the students help you create a chart to illustrate the results. Then have the students work in groups to decide which insurance company is the best. Finally, have each group present and defend its opinion.

2. After learners have completed page 19, make copies of a completed police accident report for the class. Have learners scan the report to find the answers to the following questions:

   - When did the accident occur?
   - Who was involved?
   - What happened?

Listening Script

Ted:	Hello. May I speak to Craig Anderson please?
Craig:	Speaking.
Ted:	My name is Ted Alvarez. I'm insured with 21st Century. I've just had a car accident. I've never had an accident before, so I'm not sure what to do.

Craig:	What's your insurance policy number?
Ted:	HGL-234-7895 K.
Craig:	Was anyone injured? Did the police give you a ticket?
Ted:	No. No. The accident wasn't my fault. I had stopped for a red light, but the car behind me hit me. Then I hit the car in front of me.
Craig:	Do you have the names of the drivers, their license numbers, and their insurance agents' names and phone numbers?
Ted:	No. The police officer didn't let me talk to them.
Craig:	Do you have a copy of the police report?
Ted:	No. The police officer didn't give it to me.
Craig:	Well, unfortunately, I can't do anything until I have the report. Go to the police station and ask for a copy of the report. Then fax it to me right away.
Ted:	What about my car? It was towed, and I don't have anything to drive. I had just picked up my wife from the airport when I had the accident.
Craig:	I'm afraid I can't do anything until I've looked at the police report.

Answers to Sound Bites

1. The agent asks Ted these questions:
   - What is your insurance policy number? Was anyone injured?
   - Did the police give you a ticket? Do you have the names of the other drivers? their license numbers? their insurance agents' names? a copy of the police report?

2. Ted has to fax the police report to his insurance agent.

Activity Masters

Activity Master 2-1 can be assigned anytime after the students have completed Student Book page 19 as an activity or assessment.

Presentation

1. Have the students work in groups of three and give each group a copy of Activity Master 2-1. Have the students cut out the cards, or you may want to do that ahead of time. Ask each person in the group to write a question about travel or transportation on the blank cards.

2. One person in the group collects the cards and scrambles them and puts them face down in a pile.

3. The game proceeds with the first person picking up a card and asking the second person the question on it. The second person answers the question and the third person repeats the second person's answer using reported speech.

4. Continue until all questions have been asked and answered. The round of play should go as follows:

   Person #1: How long does it take to get to school?

   Person #2: It takes me five minutes.

   Person #3: He said that it took him five minutes to get to school.

Spotlight on Present Perfect

Refer to the general instructions on page xv in the Introduction.

Presentation

1. After learners have read and discussed the examples in the Spotlight Box, have them work with a partner to use the regular and irregular verbs in the box to write sentences using present and past participles. For example, *I faxed a catalog order to a store.* OR *I have faxed many things at work.*

2. Choose one sentence for each verb to write on an overhead transparency or the board and use it to illustrate the differences between simple past tense and present perfect. Remind learners that we use present perfect to talk about things we have done in the past but may do again some time in the future.

Exercise 5

Refer to the general instructions on page xvi in the Introduction.

Answers to Exercise 5

1. faxed or sent; I haven't   2. arranged or called; I have   3. called; it hasn't

4. sent; it hasn't

Your Turn

Refer to the general instructions on page xiv in the Introduction.

Workbook

Workbook page 9 can be assigned after learners have completed Student Book page 20.

Spotlight on Past Perfect

Refer to the general instructions on page xv in the Introduction.

Preparation

Draw a time line on the board like the one in the Spotlight Box but include events and dates from your life. Then write sentences on an overhead transparency or the board to illustrate the differences among the simple past, the past perfect, and the present perfect tenses. Use the time line to help illustrate the meanings. For example, you could write the following: 1992—traveled to South America; 1998—started teaching at this school. The example sentences would look like the following:

- I traveled in South America in 1992.

- I had traveled in South America before I started teaching at this school.

- I have taught at this school since 1998.

Presentation

After learners have discussed the examples in the Spotlight Box, review the difference among the simple past, the past perfect and the present perfect. Stress that the past perfect is used to show that one action in the past happened before another action in the past. The present perfect is used to show that an action in the past relates to the present.

Exercise 6

Refer to the general instructions on page xvi in the Introduction.

Extension

For additional practice with the past perfect, duplicate a police report from a local newspaper. Have learners use the report to write sentences with present and past perfect verbs and direct and reported speech.

Answers to Exercise 6

1. had worked	4. decided	7. had stopped	10. decided
2. took	5. had earned	8. hit	11. had requested
3. had earned	6. had	9. was	12. planned

Your Turn

Refer to the general instructions on page xiv in the Introduction.

Workbook

Workbook page 10 can be assigned after learners have completed page 21.

Page 22

Get Graphic

Refer to the general instructions on page xviii in the Introduction.

Preparation

1. Duplicate train or bus maps from your local area for students to read. What features are on the maps? Have the students compare those maps in pairs or small groups with the one in Get Graphic.

2. Write the following questions on an overhead transparency (or the board) and have the students work in small groups to answer them. Have the groups share their answers with the class.
   - What is your favorite way to travel long distances? Why?
   - Which U.S. cities have you visited?
   - Which states have you visited?
   - Which city or state was your favorite place?

Exercise 7

Refer to the general instructions on page xvi in the Introduction.

Answers to Exercise 7

1. e   2. c   3. a   4. d   5. b

Exercise 8

Refer to the general instructions on page xvi in the Introduction.

Answers to Exercise 8

1. $196.00   2. $176.00   3. St. Louis and Detroit   4. Las Vegas   5. No

Extension

1. Look in your local newspaper (usually the Sunday travel section) for airfare listings and make copies for students. Have them write sentences comparing the fares in the newspaper with the fares in Get Graphic. Then have students share their sentences with the class.

2. If your class has access to the Internet, have learners use it to find out the cost of airline tickets to several destinations.

3. For more map reading and discussion practice duplicate a map of your state or region. Have learners locate places they have visited or would like to visit. Ask for volunteers to tell the class about the places they have visited. For a more structured activity, have students write questions to ask their classmates.

Page 23

Issues and Answers

Refer to the general instructions on page xix in the Introduction.

Preparation

1. Ask the students if they are familiar with advice columns in newspapers or magazines. Make sure they understand that advice columns contain letters from people asking for advice and letters back with the advice.

2. This is a good opportunity to review imperative commands and *should* and *ought to*. Explain that these modals operate the same way that the other modals they know do. These words have a base form of the verb after them and don't use *do* when forming negatives and questions. Write some examples on the board, such as the following:

   • You should talk this over with your husband.

   • You ought to try to be more patient.

Presentation

Have the students write the letter of advice individually or in pairs. Have them exchange their letters and check their partners' letters for clarity of ideas and grammatical accuracy. Then have the students write their final drafts.

Exercise 9

Refer to the general instructions on page xvi in the Introduction.

Exercise 10

Refer to the general instructions on page xvi in the Introduction.

Presentation

You may want to display the letters around the classroom for the students to read.

Extension

1. If learners enjoy reading and writing letters of advice, have them brainstorm a list of problems they have encountered that are related to the topics in this unit and write letters of advice for homework. Collect the letters, read them aloud, and ask the class to give advice.

2. Look for letters related to the topics of the unit in Ann Landers or Dear Abby and share them with the class.

Activity Masters

Activity Master 2-2 can be assigned after the students have completed Student Book page 23.

Wrap-Up

Refer to the general instructions on page xix in the Introduction.

Presentation

1. As an additional activity you may want to give each pair a transparency on which to write their responses to the questions in a chart like the one in Wrap-Up. They can refer to the chart when they report about their partners.

2. You might also tape record the learners' presentations for them to listen to at a later time.

Think About Learning

Refer to the general instructions on page xix in the Introduction.

Workbook

Workbook pages 11 and 12 can be assigned after learners have completed Student Book page 24.

ANSWERS TO PROGRESS CHECKS

Progress Check A

Speak or Write

Answers may vary. Here are some possible answers:

1. Ted is at the airport to pick up his wife, Tessa.
2. They are happy because she has returned from a trip.
3. They kiss.
4. They are going to go out for dinner. An accident changes their plans.

Listening Script

Mr. J. K. Graves of Dubuque, Iowa, had an interesting solution to a transportation problem in 1882. Dubuque is in northeastern Iowa, on the Mississippi River. There are bluffs, or tall hills, along the Mississippi there.

Graves worked at the bottom of the bluffs, but lived at the top of the bluffs. All the businesses in town closed for lunch at noon every day for an hour and a half. It took Graves half an hour to get home, half an hour to eat, half an hour to take a nap, and another half hour to return to his bank, for a total of two hours.

Graves had seen incline railways, or cable cars, in Europe, and he decided to build one in Dubuque. On July 25, 1882, Graves used his cable car for the first time. His gardener operated the car, letting Graves down in the morning, up and down at noon, and up again after work.

Neighbors started asking for rides in the car, so Graves charged them five cents for a ride. The cable car burned down several times, and each time it was rebuilt. Visitors and residents of Dubuque can still ride the car, but now it costs $1.50 for a round trip.

Listen

1. No   2. No   3. Yes   4. Yes   5. No

Progress Check B

Language Structures

1. The flight attendant announced (that) Flight 664 had just landed.

2. The bus driver said (that) this was the final boarding call.

3. The captain said (that) the ferry would be leaving in five minutes.

4. The van driver announced (that) rides from the dealer to your home were free.

5. Joe told the ticket agent (that) he wanted to buy a round-trip ticket from Chicago to New York City.

Content

1. b, d; a; c; a, c; c   2. b   3. c   4. b

ANSWERS FOR ACTIVITY MASTERS

Activity Master 2-1

Answers will vary.

Activity Master 2-2

1. False   5. False

2. True   6. False

3. True   7. False

4. False

REPRODUCIBLE MASTER
UNIT 2

WORKBOOK ANSWERS

Practice 1

1. Tim said (that) he had to get a bus transfer from the driver.

2. The clerk said (that) the train would be leaving in ten minutes.

3. My insurance agent said (that) I needed to get two copies of the report.

4. The travel agent said (that) I should bring a $200 deposit by Friday morning.

5. Jamal said (that) he was going back to Egypt.

Practice 2

1. Connie said (that) she got three weeks of vacation.

2. Mark said (that) he got four weeks of vacation.

3. Bernard said (that) he got two weeks of vacation.

Practice 3

1. The passenger said (that) he wasn't feeling well. His chest hurt.

2. The flight attendant said (that) she would see if she could find a doctor on board.

Practice 7

Answers may vary. Some possible answers are:

1. Ted had waited at the airport for an hour before the plane landed.

2. Ted and Tessa had stopped at a red light when a car hit them.

3. Ted had spoken to his insurance agent before he rented a car.

4. Ted and Tessa had requested a vacation before they made travel plans.

5. Tessa hadn't been afraid of driving before the accident.

Practice 8

1. Luz had called the office three times before she spoke to the supervisor.

2. She had had an accident when she was driving to work.

3. Her car had been towed and she needed a ride to work.

Practice 9

1. He was a businessman in Dubuque, Iowa.

2. He needed two hours for lunch so he could go home, eat, take a nap, and go back to work.

3. He built an incline railway to go back and forth from the top of the bluffs to the bottom of the bluffs.

4. It has been in use since July 25, 1882.

5. It costs $1.50 for a round-trip ticket

REPRODUCIBLE MASTER
UNIT 2

PROGRESS CHECK A

SPEAK OR WRITE

Look at the pictures from Scene 1 in Unit 2. Use the questions
below to talk or write about each picture. Retell the story in your
own words.

Questions

1. Why is Ted at the airport?

2. Are they happy? Why or why not? Explain.

3. How do Ted and his wife greet each other?

4. What are they going to do?

LISTEN

While you listen, put a check (✓) under *Yes* or *No*.

	Yes	No
1. Dubuque is the name of a river.	_____	_____
2. J. K. Graves lived at the bottom of the bluffs.	_____	_____
3. J. K. Graves went home for lunch.	_____	_____
4. J. K. Graves visited Europe.	_____	_____
5. Today, a ride on the cable car costs five cents.	_____	_____

REPRODUCIBLE MASTER

UNIT 2   PROGRESS CHECK B

LANGUAGE STRUCTURES

Change the sentences below from direct speech to reported speech.

1. The flight attendant announced, "Flight 664 has just landed."

   _____

2. The bus driver said, "This is the final boarding call."

   _____

3. The captain said, "The ferry will be leaving in five minutes."

   _____

4. The van driver announced, "Rides home are free."

   _____

5. Joe told the ticket agent, "I want a round-trip ticket from Chicago
   to New York City."

   _____

CONTENT

1. **Match Column A with Column B. Some words in Column B may
   be used twice.**

   Column A   **Column B**

   1. driver   _____   a. ferry

   2. steward   _____   b. bus

   3. flight attendant _____   c. plane

   4. captain   _____   d. van

   5. pilot   _____

2. **Circle the sentence that is not usually true about vacation requests.**
   a. Your supervisor needs to approve your vacation request.
   b. You can take as much time off as you want.

3. **Circle the place that does not have a drive-up or drive-through.**
   a. bank   b. restaurant   c. school

4. **Circle one thing to tell your insurance agent after an accident.**
   a. why you were driving   b. if you got a ticket   c. your destination

UNIT 2
ACTIVITY MASTER 2-1

THREE-WAY INTERVIEW

Directions: Work in groups of three. Follow your teacher's directions. Ask and answer the questions on the cards. Use reported speech to repeat the answers.

✂

What is your dream car?	What is one place in the world you want to visit?
What kind of transportation have you never used?	What is the most interesting place in the United States you have visited?
Have you ever been in a car accident?	When did you learn to drive?
How many times have you flown on an airplane?	
How many times a month do you ride on a bus?	
Have you ever had a speeding ticket?	

Name _____ Date _____

MORE READING FOR REAL

Read these instructions on an automobile insurance card.

This insurance card shall be displayed when requested by any law enforcement officer.

What to Do in Case of an Accident

1. Stop and Give Aid. Stop heavy bleeding, if possible. Avoid moving an injured person. It may seriously complicate the injury. Call a doctor or ambulance.

2. Warn Other Drivers to Prevent Further Damage. Set flares. Signal with a flashlight at night.

3. Notify the Police. Sometimes a passing driver or witness will do this for you.

4. Gather the Facts. Be sure to get the names of witnesses, their phone numbers, and any other important information.

5. Be Careful What You Say. Don't admit responsibility. Investigation may show you were not responsible.

6. Report the accident to Proper Authorities. Each state has its own requirements for such reports. Know the law for your state and follow it.

7. Notify Your Insurance Company Immediately. Time is important. If you can't reach your agent, telephone or fax the nearest insurance claims office listed in the telephone book.

8. Glass Repair/Replacement Claims. Call your agent before you make any repairs.

Answer the questions. Check *True* or *False*. Underline the correct information in the instructions above.

	True	False
1. Don't show your insurance card to anyone.	_____	_____
2. Use flares or a flashlight to let other cars know there has been an accident.	_____	_____
3. If you don't have a car phone, ask someone to call the police for you.	_____	_____
4. Don't talk to anyone.	_____	_____
5. Tell the police if you caused the accident.	_____	_____
6. You can wait a day or two to tell your insurance agent about the accident.	_____	_____
7. Call your agent after you make repairs.	_____	_____

UNIT 3 HELPING PEOPLE IN NEED

OVERVIEW

Objectives

Skills and Structures

Talk about people's problems

Understand recorded conversations

Read a memo and a thank-you note

Talk about how people help others

Read a bar graph and a map

Read and write letters to the editor

Brainstorm ideas about a problem and present your ideas

Use passive verbs

Use present conditionals

Use conditionals with *would*

SCANS Competencies

Participate as member of a team: Student Book, Culture Corner, page 30

Organize and maintain information: Student Book, Get Graphic, page 34; Student Book, Wrap-Up, page 36

Realia

Map of the United States

Map of Europe

Photos of natural disasters

Weather map from newspaper

Daily newspaper

Audio or video recordings of news

Bar graphs illustrating different information

ACTIVITY NOTES

Page 25

Scene 1

Preparation

1. Introduce the topic of the unit by asking the learners the following questions. Write their responses on the board.

   • What do you think the title means?

   • Who helps people in need?

   • What are some of the needs people have?

   • Have you ever helped someone in need? What did you do?

Vocabulary Prompts

Presentation

After students discuss the Vocabulary Prompts, check their understanding. Read each description or definition below and have them call out the vocabulary item it describes.

- melted rock from a volcano (lava)
- very powerful wind storm on land (tornado)
- person who works for nothing (volunteer)
- very powerful wind storm over oceans or seas (hurricane)
- a place to go for protection (shelter)

Sound Bites

While You Listen

Preparation

1. Display a large map of the United States, preferably one that shows major rivers. Show learners where North Dakota is located and ask them to tell you what they know about North Dakota. Make sure the students find the Red River. Explain that they will be hearing a conversation about the Red River. Have them think about the unit title and Scene 1 to speculate about what kind of conversation they might hear.

2. Before students listen to the Sound Bites, explain the difference between chronological order (time order) and the order in which one talks about things. To illustrate tell the students about five to seven things you did the day before. Ask students to tell you what you did first, second, third, and so on.

3. Write *destroyed, sandbags, victim, trained, disaster,* and *donate* on the board. Have students copy these words and any related words into their notebooks. Ask the class if they know what these words mean. Clarify if necessary. Have the students write the definitions or translations in their notebooks. Write *I'm really impressed* and see if the students know what it means. Have them copy it into their notebooks as well.

After You Listen

Presentation

1. After learners have told partners Gloria's story, divide the class into pairs. Play the tape or read the conversation again. Ask learners to write three to five questions about the conversation. Check the learners' questions.

2. Play the tape or read the conversation again. Have each pair choose a question to ask the class.

   Note: During the April 1997 flooding in Grand Forks, three million sand bags were filled according to the Chicago Tribune (April 28, 1998). Sandbags that were touched by the river waters were taken to landfills. The untouched bags were donated for use in the community.

Extension

Look in the newspaper or use the Internet for stories that mention the Red Cross. Bring the stories to class and share them with learners.

 Option 1: Have learners work in groups. Give each group a story to read. Write the headlines for each story on an overhead transparency or the board. Pair the groups and have each group write a list of three or four questions to ask about the other story. Then have those groups get together and ask and answer questions about the stories they read.

Option 2: If you have several stories, divide the class into groups and give each group a story to read and discuss. Have the students write a summary of the story. Copy the summaries on an overhead transparency and discuss which summary is the best.

Option 3: If learners have Internet access, have them look for stories about the Red Cross to share. Many libraries have CD-ROMS of local newspapers, as well as encyclopedias. Some libraries also have computers with Internet access.

Listening Script

Juana:	I missed you last week, Gloria. Were you on vacation?
Gloria:	Well, I took the week off, but I wasn't really on vacation.
Juana:	I don't understand.
Gloria:	You know about the flooding along the Red River in North Dakota and all the homes that were destroyed, don't you?
Juana:	Sure. But what does that have to do with you?
Gloria:	Well, I was one of the Red Cross volunteers there. On the first day, enough sandbags were filled to make a three-foot high wall, and meals were served to more than a hundred flood victims. I passed out blankets at a shelter in a high school.
Juana:	Why did you do that?
Gloria:	When I was a child in Colombia, my village was destroyed by a volcano. The houses were covered with lava and ashes, and many people were killed. I remembered the kindness of the Red Cross volunteers, so when I heard about the flooding, I volunteered to help.
Juana:	I'm really impressed.
Gloria:	Well, don't be. It makes me feel good to help other people. You know, there are about 10 million Red Cross volunteers in the United States, and I don't know how many in 134 other countries.
Juana:	Ten million!
Gloria:	Sure. Red Cross volunteers do many things. They are trained to provide all kinds of help to disaster victims. You know—victims of floods, tornadoes, earthquakes, hurricanes. The Red Cross offers classes in first-aid and water safety. Volunteers also teach health classes, serve in military hospitals, and donate blood.
Juana:	How did you find out about all of this?
Gloria:	From a volunteer fair I went to a year ago at my son's school.

Answers to Sound Bites

a. 6   b. 3   c. 2   d.   e. 4   f. 5

Page 27

Spotlight on the Passive Voice

Preparation

1. After learners have read and discussed the examples in the Spotlight Box, use the examples and ask the following questions for each sentence:

   - What is the subject?
   - What is the action?
   - Is the subject doing the action?
   - What is the action?
   - Is the subject receiving the action?

2. Help learners distinguish between passive and active verbs by reminding them that when the subject of the verb is the doer of the action, the verb is active. When the subject of the verb receives the action, the verb is passive.

Exercise 1

Extension

1. If learners are interested in Clara Barton or Jean Henri Dunant, have them look for more information about them at the library. Ask learners to share information with the class.

 Option 1: Have less advanced learners write five sentences about either Clara Barton or Jean Henri Dunant.

Option 2: Have students write a short summary of either Clara Barton's or Jean Henri Dunant's lives.

Option 3: Have students work in pairs and pretend to be on a talk show. On person pretends to be a news interviewer. The other is either Clara Barton or Jean Henri Dunant. Have the interviewer ask questions about the person's life. The "person" should answer appropriately according to the information found in the research. You may want to videotape the interviews as a talk show.

2. Collect newspaper stories that use passive verbs. Select stories that might be of interest to learners. Photocopy the stories and have learners work in groups or pairs, and ask them to underline the verbs they find, decide if the verbs are active or passive, and rewrite sentences with passive verbs, making them active. Ask each group to read one or more of their sentences (passive to active) to the rest of the class.

Answers to Exercise 1

1. A   2. P   3. A   4. A   5. A   6. A   7. P   8. P

Answers to Your Turn

People all over the world are helped by the Red Cross in times of war and peace.

A battlefield in Italy was visited by Dunant in 1859.

No one was seen helping the wounded soldiers.

Dunant wanted to help people, so the Red Cross was started.

Person to Person

Extension

1. Have learners work in pairs to identify and underline the passive verbs.

2. Write the questions from the Preparation for the Spotlight Box on page 27 on an overhead transparency or the board.

3. Have learners ask each other those questions using the verbs in Person to Person so they can reinforce their understanding of the difference between active and passive verbs.

4. Ask volunteers to rewrite the three sentences with passive verbs from the conversations on the board.

Workbook

Workbook pages 13 and 14 may be assigned after learners have completed Student Book page 28.

Reading for Real

Preparation

1. Ask learners with jobs to bring memos or newsletters from their workplaces which relate to helping others. If possible, use the information for a class discussion after learners have talked about fires and helping other people. Ask learners who work how they feel about asking for help from people at work or giving help to people at work.

2. Review chronological order.

Exercise 2

Extension

For additional practice with passive verbs, have learners work with partners to rewrite the sentences in Exercise 2 from passive to active. Ask volunteers to write the sentences on the board.

Answers to Exercise 2

1. A fire was started by a faulty water heater.
2. A home was destroyed by a fire.
3. The Flash Cable Company was notified about the fire.
4. Money, clothing, household goods, and furniture were given to the family.
5. Donations were received by the family.
6. A thank-you note was sent to employees.

Culture Corner

Preparation

Invite one or more volunteers from the learners' community to class to be interviewed by them. Have the learners prepare questions ahead of time and practice them with a partner before the interviews.

Exercise 3

Extension

1. After the interviews, have learners write thank-you notes to the volunteers. You may want to prepare a simple form for learners to follow.

2. Look in the local newspapers for volunteer opportunities. Bring the information to class and discuss it.

Scene 2

Preparation

Lead a discussion about tornadoes. Display any photos of tornadoes you have. Have the students describe what they know about them by asking the following questions:

- Who knows what a tornado is? Has anyone ever seen a movie about a tornado? Which one?
- What part of the United States do most of the tornadoes occur (the Midwest)
- What kind of damage do you think a tornado can do?

Extension

After learners have discussed Scene 2, and if you live in an area where tornadoes are common, have a brief class discussion about tornado safety. Many schools routinely have tornado drills, so your adult learners should be aware of safety precautions. If your school does not have written tornado instructions, make a class list of things to do if there is a tornado. (Open the windows, close the outside doors, go to the lowest place in the interior of the building and crouch on the floor with your hands behind you head. Stay away from windows.)

Sound Bites

While You Listen

Preparation

1. Have the students work in small groups to brainstorm a list of disasters. Have the students make T-charts in their notebooks and write their ideas in the chart. They should head one column of the T-chart *Natural Disasters* and the other column *Disasters Caused by People*. Display the photos of natural disasters.

2. Write *occurred, collision, erupt, resident, evacuate, explode,* and *debris* on the board. Have students copy these words and any related words into their notebooks. Ask the class if they know what these words mean. Clarify if necessary. Have the students write the definitions or translations in their notebooks.

Extension

Tape record or video record several weather-related news stories or stories about disasters. While learners listen to the tapes, have them fill in a chart like the one in While You Listen.

Listening Script

1. A terrible traffic accident occurred today at 4:00 P.M. on Interstate 80. Sudden ice and snow caused a 55-vehicle collision. Ice-covered roads caused the multiple accidents. Fifteen people were killed. Our reporter interviewed one of the drivers. The driver said, "It was terrible. I couldn't see anything, so I started to slow down. I couldn't see the car in front of me until I hit it. If I know the roads are bad, I stay home."

2. This is John Porter reporting from Mexico. In the background I can see the volcano, El Popo, throwing smoke and ash into the air. Cars, trucks, bicycles, and people are on the roads leading away from the erupting volcano. This active volcano has threatened to destroy this town for years. If I were a gambler, I'd bet this is it!

3. Residents of Kitty Hawk, North Carolina, are preparing for the worst hurricane in twenty years. One-hundred-fifty-mile-per-hour winds are heading our way. Most of the residents have evacuated already. But there are always a few who refuse to leave their homes no matter what. They must be crazy, if they aren't afraid of this storm!

4. This report just came in from Paris. A bomb has exploded in a crowded market-place. Over 150 people are dead or wounded. At this time, it is unknown who set off the bomb or why. Debris and smoke are everywhere. You can hear the screams and cries of the injured. One of the firefighters on the scene said, "The destruction is unbelievable. I don't understand why this happened. If I could, I'd leave the country right now."

Answers to Sound Bites

1. traffic accident—Interstate 80

2. volcano eruption—Mexico

3. evacuation for hurricane—Kitty Hawk, North Carolina

4. bomb explosion—Paris

Page 32

Spotlight on Present Conditional

Preparation

1. Review the differences between words, phrases, clauses, and sentences. Put the following examples on the board and have learners tell you how the four examples differ.

   • Midwest (word)

   • in the Midwest (phrase)

   • If you live in the Midwest, (clause)

   • You can expect tornadoes. (sentence)

2. Write, "If you live in the Midwest, you can expect tornadoes" on the board. Tell learners you have combined a clause (subject, verb, but not a complete idea) with a sentence (subject, verb, complete idea). Stress that the sentence can stand alone, but the clause cannot. Explain that when the *if* clause begins the sentence, it must be followed by a comma.

Exercise 4

Extension

Have the learners work in pairs to write a conversation about the weather. Have them use the factual conditional. Circulate among the students to make sure they use the factual conditional correctly. Then have the pairs present their conversations to the class.

 Option 1: Have less advanced students write a five line conversation about the weather.

Option 2: Ask students to watch or listen to the weather news on the radio or TV. Have them write a summary of the day's weather and the forecast for the rest of the week.

Option 3: Have the students work in pairs to create a TV weather report. They should have a detailed weather forecast with a map to illustrate the weather patterns. Have them watch actual TV news weather reports to get ideas. Make sure that both people in each pair have a chance to do the reporting. Videotape the weather reports.

Answers to Exercise 4

1. c   2. e   3. a   4. b   5. d

Page 33

Spotlight on Conditional with *Would*

Preparation

1. Contrary-to-fact or untrue conditionals use the past tense of the verb in a present or future sense. In some formal English, the subjunctive is used. For example, "If I were President, I would eliminate taxes." Write the following list of sentence beginnings on the board. Ask learners if these clauses are true or unlikely.

    - If animals talked,
    - If pigs flew,
    - If money grew on trees,
    - If wishes were dollars,

2. Have learners work with a partner to complete the sentences. Ask for volunteers to read their sentences to the class.

Workbook

Workbook pages 15 and 16 can be assigned after learners have completed Student Book page 33.

Activity Masters

Activity Master 3-1 can be assigned after learners have completed pages 15 and 16 in the Workbook.

Presentation

1. Duplicate enough copies of the Activity Master so that each student has one card. Cut the cards apart and give each learner a card with the beginning or the ending of a sentence.

2. Have learners walk around the room and read their sentence parts to each other. Ask learners to sit down together when they find a match. You may want to time this activity.

3. Have each pair read its sentence to the rest of the class. The class decides if the parts match.

Page 34

Get Graphic

Preparation

1. Explain to the learners that bar graphs are another way to illustrate quantities. Have them compare the bar graph with the graph in Unit 2, page 22.

2. Bring in a variety of bar graphs and have the students determine what quantities these graphs are illustrating.

Exercise 6

Extension

Look in your local newspaper for weather-related charts and graphs to share with the class. Have learners work in pairs of groups to prepare questions about the information in the graphs. Have learners in one group exchange graphs with another pair or group and ask and answer the questions.

Answers to Exercise 6

1. Illinois   2. Ohio   3. April, May, June

4. February   5. December, January, February

Brain Teaser: Temperatures fluctuate, or go up and down. The weather conditions and temperatures are unstable or change quickly.

Activity Masters

Activity Master 3-2 can be assigned after learners have completed Student Book page 34.

Page 35

Issues and Answers

Preparation

Ask learners if they know what the letters the editor section of a newspaper is. Ask volunteers to describe it. Have the students identify if the following statements are true or false:

- The letters to the editor are opinions of the newspaper. (false)
- The letters to the editor are guaranteed factual. (false)
- The letters are published so that a variety of opinions and issues can be made known. (true)

Answers to Exercise 7

Answers will vary. Possible answers include the following:

Krystyna Machalek: There has been terrible flooding in Poland, and the paper is not giving the situation the coverage it deserves.

Joan Shipley: Last week was National Volunteer Week and the paper didn't mention it at all and therefore neglected to recognize the many volunteers in the city. The paper should write more about volunteers.

Page 36

Workbook

Workbook pages 17 and 18 can be assigned after students have completed Student Book page 36.

ANSWERS TO PROGRESS CHECKS

Progress Check A

Speak or Write

Answers will vary but may include the following:

1. A tornado has occurred.
2. There is little that could have been done to prevent property damage because people didn't have enough warning ahead of time to do anything.
3. After tornadoes, volunteers can help clean up, feed people, run shelters, give blood, and so on.
4. People help because they have good hearts. Sometimes they help because other people have helped them in the past.

Listening Script

The British government is closing evacuation shelters on the island of Montserrat. The Soufriere Hills volcano continues to threaten the safety of residents on this tiny island in the Caribbean. The volcano has already destroyed two-thirds of the island. Last year most residents left the capital city because of volcanic eruptions.

 The government wants people to leave the island. They are offering about $4,000 to every adult who leaves. Residents can have housing for three weeks on the nearby island of Antigua. Then they will have to decide where to go next.

 About 2,000 people are still living in temporary shelters on the island. The volcano killed 20 people in June. Montserrat is about the size of Washington, D.C.

Listen

1. b   2. b   3. b   4. a   5. a

Progress Check B

Language Structures

1. A Thousands of power lines were knocked down by a winter ice storm in the Northeastern United States and Canada.
2. A Fourteen deaths were caused by the storm.
3. P Officials urged people to go to emergency shelters.
4. Answers will vary.
5. Answers will vary.

Content

1. c   2. c   3. b   4. b   5. b

ANSWERS ACTIVITY MASTERS

Activity Master 3-1

1. If you are healthy, you can be a blood donor.
2. If you like to cook, you can prepare food at a homeless shelter.
3. If you are friendly and like older people, you can volunteer at a senior citizens center.
4. If you're good at sports, you can coach youth athletics.
5. I might be a lawyer if I had the time and money to go back to school.
6. If I had a college degree, I'd be a teacher.
7. If I owned a business, I'd give my employees cash bonuses on their birthdays.
8. If I had a new car, I'd drive to Mexico to visit my family.
9. Don't be a scout leader if you don't like children.
10. Don't volunteer to deliver meals to seniors if your car isn't dependable.

Activity Master 3-2

Answers will vary.

REPRODUCIBLE MASTER
UNIT 3

WORKBOOK ANSWERS

Practice 1

1. **A** flowed

2. **P** were destroyed

3. **A** said

4. **P** were burned

5. **A** killed, swept

6. **A** erupt

7. **A** has been abandoned

8. **A** used to live

Practice 2

Answers will vary. Possible answers include the following:

2. Fire destroyed a church, a clothing store, a supermarket, and a dozen houses.

4. This is the first time a volcano burned buildings in Plymouth.

5. Most of the time since then, people have abandoned Plymouth.

Practice 6

1. e   2. g   3. h   4. c   5. f   6. a   7. b   8. d

Practice 10

1. She is the director of the Impact India Foundation.

2. He wanted to bring doctors to people in rural areas.

3. First she lent him a surgical van. Then she raised money to buy a train.

4. It's a hospital train.

5. She wants to develop a three-story hospital boat in Bangladesh.

Name _____ Date _____

UNIT 3   PROGRESS CHECK A

SPEAK OR WRITE

Look at the pictures from Unit 3. Use the questions below to talk or
write about each. Retell the story in your own words.

Questions

1. What natural disaster has occurred?

2. Could anything have been done to prevent damage to people or
   property? Why or why not?

3. What things can volunteers do to help after this natural disaster?

4. Why do you think people volunteer to help others after natural
   disasters?

LISTEN

While you listen, circle the correct answer.

1. Montserrat is in _____.
   a. the Pacific Ocean   b. the Caribbean

2. The British Government wants people to _____.
   a. stay on the island   b. leave the island

3. The government is giving people _____.
   a. $400   b. $4,000

4. There are _____ people on the island.
   a. 2000   b. 200

5. Montserrat is the size of _____.
   a. Washington, D.C.   b. Iowa

Name _____ Date _____

PROGRESS CHECK B

LANGUAGE STRUCTURES

Underline the verbs. Write *A* if the verb is active and *P* if the verb is passive. Re-write the sentences. Change the active verbs to passive and the passive verbs to active.

1. _____ A winter ice storm knocked down thousands of power lines in the Northeastern United States and Canada.

   _____

2. _____ The storm caused 14 deaths.

   _____

3. _____ People were urged by officials to go to emergency shelters.

   _____

Complete the sentences below.

4. If a volcano erupts, _____

5. I might speak English better if I _____

CONTENT

Circle the correct answers.

1. The Red Cross is a _____.
   a. a restaurant   b. a club   c. an organization

2. Red Cross members don't _____.
   a. give blood   b. clean up after disasters   c. sell food

3. Volunteers _____.
   a. expect to be paid   b. work for free   c. accept tips

4. Which of the following is not a natural disaster?
   a. flood   b. plane crash   c. earthquake

5. If you lived in the Midwest, what natural disaster could you expect in April, May, or June?
   a. tidal wave   b. tornado   c. hurricane

ACTIVITY MASTER 3-1

MATCH UP

See page 55 of the Teacher's Manual for complete directions on this activity.

Column A	Column B
If you are healthy,	you can be a blood donor.
If you like to cook,	you can prepare food at a homeless shelter.
If you are friendly and like older people,	you can volunteer at a senior citizens' center.
If you're good at sports,	you can coach youth athletics.
I might be a lawyer	if I had the time and money to go back to school.
If I had a college degree,	I'd be a teacher.
If I owned a business,	I'd give my employees cash bonuses on their birthdays.
If I had a new car,	I'd drive to Mexico to visit my family.
Don't be a scout leader	if you don't like children.
Don't volunteer to deliver meals to seniors	if your car isn't dependable.

Name _____ Date _____

MORE GRAPHIC SKILLS

Work with a group. Read the table.

Some Floods to Remember

Date	Location	Deaths
June 9, 1972	Rapid City, South Dakota	236
July 31, 1976	Big Thompson Canyon, Colorado	139
July 19–20, 1979	Johnstown, Pennsylvania	68
Aug. 11, 1979	Morvi, India	15,000
Sept. 17–21, 1982	El Salvador, Guatemala	1,300
July 19, 1985	Dam Collapse, Northern Italy	361
July, 1995	Hunan Province, India	1,200
June–July, 1996	South China	315
March, 1997	Ohio River Valley,	35
July, 1997	Poland, Czech Republic	98

As a group, write five questions about the table. Give the questions to another group to answer. Check the group's answers.

1. _____

_____

2. _____

_____

3. _____

_____

4. _____

_____

5. _____

_____

ALTERNATIVE MEDICINE AND HEALTHY LIVING

OVERVIEW

Objectives

Skills and Structures

Talk about health problems

Understand medical recordings

Understand alternative medicine and health insurance

Read a medical statement

Understand health statistics

Read and write suggestions

Use an idea map about health in different cultures

Use gerunds and infinitives

SCANS Competencies

Acquire and evaluate information: Student Book, Sound Bites, page 38; Student Book, Student Book, Reading for Real, page 41; Sound Bites, page 43; Workbook, Read, Think, and Write, page 23

Solve problems: Student Book, Issues and Answers, page 47

Self-manage: Teacher's Manual, Activity Master 4-2

Realia

Holistic magazines and articles dealing with alternative medicine

Examples of health statements (bills) and health plan policies, particularly pages dealing with covered and uncovered medical procedures

Health pamphlets on how to prevent the spread of HIV/AIDS or reduce the risk of heart disease

ACTIVITY NOTES

Page 37

Scene I

Preparation

1. As a baseline for comparison, ask students to compare doctors and medical practices in their countries versus those in the United States. Set up a simple chart with two headings: *Medicine in the United States* and *Medicine in My Native Country*. Students can brainstorm the differences. Ask, "Is taking medicine the only way to get better when you're sick or unhealthy?" With the class make a list of other ways to keep healthy.

2. Discuss the differences between Western medicine and alternative medicine in the United States. Have students relate types of medicine from their native countries that might be considered alternative medicine in the United States.

Sound Bites

While You Listen

Preparation

1. With your students brainstorm a list of possible reasons a person might call a doctor's office or a health insurance company.

2. Write *resource, potential, extension, respiratory, nutrition,* and *life-threatening* on the board. Have students copy these words and any related words into their notebooks. Ask the class if they know what these words mean. Clarify if necessary. Have the students write the definitions or translations in their notebooks.

Extension

1. Make a recording of menu selections for a health plan or hospital. Play the recording and ask students to tell you which numbers they would press for a given option. For example, to reach the lab, what number should they press?

2. Have learners work in pairs to discuss what information or advice each caller might get. Have them speculate on what they think will happen next in each situation.

3. Have the learners work in groups to talk about calls they have made for medical services. Model the activity by saying why you called and whether it was easy or difficult to get help.

Listening Script

1. You have reached the Alternative Medical Group, your number one resource in developing human potential and wellness. If you know your party's extension, you may dial at any time. For lower back and neck pain, press *one* to speak to a chiropractor. For respiratory conditions such as asthma and allergies, press *two* to speak to an acupuncturist. If you want to order a schedule of our yoga, meditation, or nutrition classes, press *three*. To speak to a receptionist, please continue to hold.

2. You have reached the Family Doctors Center. If this is a life-threatening emergency, please press *one*. To make, reschedule, or cancel an appointment, please press *two*. For a nurse's advice, please press *three*. For all other calls, please press *four*. If you belong to an HMO or PPO, please remember to have your medical record number ready. . . Flu season is upon us. If you're over 65, don't delay getting that flu shot!

3. You have reached the administrative offices of Atlantic HMO. We're sorry, but all our representatives are busy. Your call is very important to us. Please continue holding, and your call will be answered in the order in which it was received. To listen to our department directory, press *one*. To enroll in the health plan, press *two*. To select a primary care physician, press *three*. To discuss a bill, press *four*. We believe in giving quality care at Atlantic HMO.

Answers to Sound Bites

1. 2, 1   2. 3, 1   3. 2, 4

Spotlight on Gerunds

Preparation

1. Introduce the idea of gerunds as subjects by writing the following unfinished sentences on the blackboard:

   • _____ lots of fat isn't good for you.

   • _____ water is very healthy for you.

   • _____ exercise is very important.

2. Ask students to supply the missing verbs (*eating, drinking,* and *doing*). Ask students to list more health tips along these lines, using gerunds as subjects.

3. Introduce gerunds as objects by talking about what sports and exercise students like or dislike. In small groups, students talk or write, using these sentence starters. Have students report the results back to the class.

   I like (playing/doing/watching) _____

   I don't like (playing/doing/watching) _____

Answers to Exercise 1

1. T   2. T   3. F   4. T   5. T   6. F   7. T

Workbook

Workbook pages 19 and 20 can be assigned after students have completed Student Book page 39.

Person to Person

Preparation

Review the discussion you had with the students about alternative medicine. Write different kinds of alternative medicine across the top of an overhead transparency or on the board. Ask students what kind of activities go with each kind of medicine. Write the activities under each type of alternative medicine.

Extension

Ask the class to make a list of home remedies using the following structures. Enjoy the variety of surprising advice and the cultural exchange that will likely result!

Drinking milk can help you to sleep.

    (gerund)   (infinitive)

For a stomachache, try eating cumin.

    (problem)   (gerund)

 Option 1: Have students perform the dialogues using the lines written. You can assign pairs or let students choose their own partners.

Option 2: Have students write the next couple of lines for each dialogue. Then have them present their dialogues to the class. You may want to videotape their conversations.

Option 3: More advanced students can write additional dialogues for each conversation. This second dialogue should be between the patient and the health-care practitioner. Encourage them to use gerunds in their conversations. Have the students present their dialogues to the class. You may want to videotape their presentations.

Answers to Person to Person

Answers may vary. Here are some possible answers: garlic, zinc, ginseng.

Reading for Real

Preparation

Bring in examples of health insurance statements. Ask the following questions:

- What is the statement saying?
- Do you owe money or not?
- What services is the statement for?
- Has your insurance company paid its share? How much did it pay?
- Who do you call if you have questions?

Answers to Exercise 2

1. Healthsource   2. 12/6/98   3. $14.00   4. $00.00
5. Answers may vary. Here are some possible answers: Pay the bill. OR Call and ask why acupuncture was not paid for.

Culture Corner

Extension

Have the class make a bulletin board with advertisements and articles from holistic health magazines. Encourage students to bring in articles about exercise, healthy living, and so forth. Students can also report on Health Watch portions of the nightly TV news. Ask the following questions:

- What are some current health issues in the United States?
- What are solutions to some of those problems?

Scene 2

Preparation

Quickly review the story line from Scene 1. Kamal has bad allergies and his medicine only puts him to sleep. His coworker asks if he's tried alternative medicine like acupuncture. Kamal is desperate and willing to try anything at this point.

Sound Bites

While You Listen

Preparation

1. Ask the class if anyone has ever had to talk to someone from a health insurance company. Have the person share the experience.

   - Who did you call?
   - Why did you call?
   - Was the person at the insurance company helpful and nice?
   - Was your problem solved?

2. Write *claims form, required, policy handbook,* and *treatment* on the board. Have students copy these words and any related words into their notebooks. Ask the class if they know what these words mean. Clarify if necessary. Have the students write the definitions or translations in their notebooks.

Extension

Have learners research the health resources in their local community. Where can students see a doctor or dentist? Are there any free or low-cost services? Are there health services at the educational institution itself? Have students share their knowledge, particularly of bilingual doctors and services.

 Option 1: Have students look in the yellow pages of the phone book to make a list of the different kinds of services available.

Option 2: Have students pick one or two places that offer alternative medicine from the phone book to call. Have them find information on whether insurance is accepted, how much treatments cost, and what is needed to be evaluated by a health care practitioner in that office.

Option 3: If appropriate, take a tour of a nearby health facility or clinic. Inquire about free wellness screenings or health-related lectures for your class or school.

Listening Script

Representative:	Customer service. May I help you?
Kamal:	Yes, this is Kamal Patel. I had acupuncture on January 15 for some terrible allergies.
Representative:	Uh-huh.
Kamal:	And I filled out all the claim forms, but I still got a statement saying that I need to pay the whole bill.
Representative:	That's because . . .
Kamal:	I thought the health plan paid for all my doctor appointments.
Representative:	The only way . . .
Kamal:	I know—I was supposed to see my primary doctor.
Representative:	That's right.
Kamal:	But I already went to him, and all he did was give me medicine that put me to sleep.

Representative:	Well, if you want to see a specialist, you are required to get a referral. Have you read the policy handbook?
Kamal:	Yes, I have now. Will the plan pay for acupuncture? I think it might really help my allergies.
Representative:	Well . . . as a matter of fact, there are some primary care physicians who have approved experimental treatments before.
Kamal:	Really?
Representative:	Yes, and you can change doctors.
Kamal:	I can? That would be great.
Representative:	But you may have a waiting period.
Kamal:	That's all right.
Representative:	Here, let me pull up the list of physicians on my computer.

Answers to Sound Bites

Answers may vary. Here are some possible answers.

Kamal is frustrated because the phone menu is not easy to understand. He wants to know if the health plan will pay for the acupuncture. The person tells him that he should have gotten a referral, but that some primary care physicians have approved experimental treatments before. He can change doctors, but there may be a waiting period. The representative gives him a list of physicians.

Page 44

Spotlight on Infinitives

Preparation

1. Introduce the verb + infinitive structure by writing these unfinished sentences on the board. Ask students to write endings to the following:

   • I want to _____.

   • I need to _____.

   • I hope to _____.

2. Explain that verbs such as these must be followed by an infinitive (*to* form of the verb), not a gerund (*-ing* form of the verb). You may want students to get into small groups and finish the above sentence starters, to give the future direction of the infinitives in these constructions. Students can talk about things they want, need or hope to do.

Answers to Exercise 3

Answers may vary. Here are some possible answers:

1. to get/to have   2. to see/to go to   3. to get   4. to have

5. to make   6. to go 7. to have   8. to do

Spotlight on Gerunds and Infinitives

Preparation

1. To contrast the three structures (verb followed by infinitive only, gerund only, and infinitive or gerund), ask learners to complete the following sentences with the phrase *get exercise:*

   - I suggest _____
   - I need _____
   - I like _____

2. Explain that learning which verbs take gerunds, infinitives, or either one takes practice and time. Let learners know that some very fluent nonnative speakers still have trouble with gerunds and infinitives. Practice hearing, reading, and using these structures will make them familiar to learners.

3. Below is a short list of some commonly used verbs and the structure they take. Think of creative ways to use these lists in subsequent classes, perhaps by introducing a few in each class, having two-minute pop-quizzes or staging competitions.

   - Verbs with gerunds: *avoid, enjoy, give up, keep (on), mind, postpone, risk, stop, suggest*
   - Verbs with infinitives: *decide, forget, hope, know how, learn, refuse*
   - Verbs with gerunds or infinitives: *afford, begin, continue, hate, like, love, plan, prefer, remember, start, try*

Answers to Exercise 4

1. seeing	2. joining	3. having	4. to work/working
5. to choose	6. having	7. to make	8. to speak	9. to get

Workbook

Workbook pages 21 and 22 may be assigned after students have completed Student Book page 45.

Activity Masters

Activity Master 4-1 can be assigned after students have completed Student Book page 45.

Presentation

1. Have the learners work in groups of three. Duplicate a copy of Activity 4-1 for each group. Cut out the cards or have the students do it. Have the learners place the cards face down in two separate piles—an A pile and a B pile.

2. Explain that person 1 picks up a card from each pile and tries to form a true, correct sentence using a gerund or infinitive (or both) with the B verb.

3. The other two people in the group listen and help correct if necessary. Sentences must make sense! (If necessary, provide a key for the listeners indicating whether the target verbs take gerunds, infinitives, or both.)

4. When the piles are finished, separate them again, shuffle, and keep going.

5. You may want to make this a class competition between two teams. Each correct sentence is worth one point. The team with the most points wins.

   Here is an example: A verb: *need*   B verb: *see*
   Possible sentence: "I'll need to see a dentist. My tooth hurts."

Get Graphic

Preparation

1. Ask the class if anyone knows what statistics are. Clarify if necessary. Explain why statistics are important in analyzing situations. Have the class brainstorm a list of different kinds of statistics that they have been involved with (census, TV programming preferences, immigration, and so forth).

Answers to Exercise 5

1. c   2. e   3. a   4. d   5. b

Answers to Exercise 6

1. true   2. false   3. true   4. true   5. false

Workbook

Workbook pages 24 and 25 can be assigned after students have completed Student Book page 46.

Issues and Answers

Preparation

Lead a discussion about suggestion boxes at work. Ask the following questions:

- Do companies have suggestion boxes in your native country?
- If you want to make a suggestion to improve something at work in your native country, how do you do it?
- Is there any kind of negative consequence for making a constructive suggestion that may go against the policies already in place?

Extension

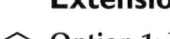 **Option 1:** Institute a suggestion box in your ESL classroom! Each week, pick a few suggestions, read them to the class, and discuss how to resolve issues or respond to suggestions.

Option 2: Have students write a health-related problem anonymously and the person who responds reads the problem and suggestion aloud.

Option 3: Have each student write a health-related problem on an index card and sign his or her name. Collect the index cards and distribute them randomly around the class. Other students write suggestions and return the cards to the writers.

Wrap-Up

Extension

If possible, involve learners in the production of the health newsletter. If computers are available, have students type their paragraphs and add graphics. Use the newsletter as a reading text and a springboard for future discussion and grammar focus activities.

Activity Masters

Activity Master 4-2 can be assigned after students have completed Student Book page 48.

ANSWERS TO PROGRESS CHECKS

Progress Check A

Speak or Write

Answers will vary. Some possible answers are the following:

1. He's unhappy because he's frustrated.

2. He has allergy medicine, but it just makes him sleepy.

3. He might take the suggestion seriously. He'll try anything at this point.

Listening Script

Reporter:	Dr. Feelgood, please tell us how to live a healthier life.
Doctor:	Well, first we've got to become aware of all the dangerous chemicals in our food and in our homes.
Reporter:	What chemicals are in our food?
Doctor:	There are chemicals in meat, and many fruits and vegetables are full of pesticides.
Reporter:	Chemical pesticides?
Feelgood:	Yes, chemicals sprayed on plants to kill bugs and insects.
Reporter:	I see.
Doctor:	I suggest buying only organic fruits and vegetables. These have no pesticides sprayed on them.
Reporter:	Don't they cost more?
Doctor:	Yes, but pesticides could give you cancer. Isn't preventing that disease worth the extra money?
Reporter:	Yes, well . . . could you tell us about the other dangers in our homes?
Doctor:	Well, there are electromagnetic toxins.
Reporter:	Do you mean from electric waves?

Doctor: Yes, electric waves from alarm clocks, microwave ovens, and hair dryers . . . these can hurt our bodies too.

Reporter: Well, Dr. Feelgood, we've run out of time. Thanks for the advice on healthy living!

Listen

1. No 2. Yes 3. Yes 4. No 5. No

Progress Check B

Language Structures

1. learning
2. to try
3. having/to have
4. taking
5. having/to have
6. paying
7. to continue

Content

1. d 2. b 3. b 4. c

ANSWERS TO ACTIVITY MASTERS

Activity Master 4-1

Answers will vary.

Activity Master 4-2

1. True 2. False 3. False 4. False 5. True

Workbook Answers

Practice 1

1. Understanding   2. Eating   3. Exercising   4. Paying   5. Seeing

Practice 2

1. thinking   2. living   3. choosing   4. worrying   5. seeing

Practice 3

1. Women should quit smoking before they are pregnant.

2. Avoid taking this medicine when you are driving.

3. Consider asking your doctor about alternative medicines.

4. May I suggest seeing someone who does acupuncture?

Practice 4

1. to relax 2. to learn 3. to speak 4. to make 5. to bring 6. to get 7. to take 8. to see

Practice 5

1. filling; I hate to fill out insurance forms.

2. having; Toni doesn't like to have to get a referral from her doctor.

3. cooking; Carol Anne likes to cook healthy meals for her family.

4. talking; The nurse said she'll continue to talk about herbal medicines next week.

Practice 7

1. Health Maintenance Organization; a large system of medical services

2. Preferred Provider Organization; a large system of medical services that is similar to an HMO because members pay fixed or small amounts.

3. Answers will vary.

Name _____ Date _____

SPEAK OR WRITE

Look at the pictures from Unit 4. Use the questions below to talk or write about each picture. Retell the story in your own words.

Questions

1. Why is Kamal unhappy?

2. What is wrong with how Kamal is taking care of himself now?

3. What does Kamal think of Jay's suggestion?

4. Do you think Jay's suggestion will help Kamal? Why or why not?

LISTEN

While you listen, check the correct answer.

	Yes	No
1. Dr. Feelgood is talking to a patient.	_____	_____
2. The doctor is talking about how to live a healthy life.	_____	_____
3. There are chemicals in our food.	_____	_____
4. Organic foods aren't worth the cost.	_____	_____
5. Pesticides are electric waves.	_____	_____

UNIT 4   PROGRESS CHECK B

LANGUAGE STRUCTURES

First read the story. Then write the verb in the correct form: as a gerund (*-ing*), an infinitive (*to . . .*), or both.

Carmelo had terrible nose congestion. He had surgery in his country, but it didn't help. When he moved to the United States, he became interested in (1) *learn* _____ about alternative medicine. He decided (2) *try* _____ acupuncture. He began (3) *have* _____ treatments every week. His doctor suggested (4) *take* _____ Chinese herbs, too. He continued (5) *have* _____ acupuncture for six months. He felt better, but he didn't like (6) *pay* _____ the bills. He had to stop the acupuncture. He wants (7) *continue* _____ his treatments, but he can't afford it now.

CONTENT

1. In _____, the doctor moves the body into different positions.
   - a. acupuncture
   - b. aromatherapy
   - c. ayurveda
   - d. chiropractic

2. _____ is based on our sense of smell.
   - a. Acupuncture
   - b. Aromatherapy
   - c. Ayurveda
   - d. Chiropractic

3. In a(n) _____ you can choose any doctor.
   - a. HMO
   - b. PPO
   - c. referral
   - d. primary-care physician

4. In some health plans you need a(n) _____ to see a specialist.
   - a. HMO
   - b. PPO
   - c. referral
   - d. primary-care physician

Name _____   Date _____

REPRODUCIBLE MASTER
UNIT 4

ACTIVITY MASTER 4-1

THREE-WAY PRACTICE WITH GERUNDS AND INFINITIVES

Note: See Teacher's Manual page 70 for complete directions on this activity.

✂

(A) appreciate	(B) have
(A) suggest	(B) see
(A) decide	(B) go
(A) need	(B) get
(A) want	(B) take
(A) like	(B) learn
(A) hate	(B) look for
(A) start	(B) talk to

© NTC/Contemporary Publishing Group, Inc.

MORE READING FOR REAL

How to Control Stress

Stress can make you tense, unhappy, and even ill. Here are some ways to control it.

1. **Let Go**   Stop trying to do too many things. Stop rushing from place to place. Organize your schedule so you can get around without rushing. If it's not important, don't do it. Stop worrying and try to enjoy your life more.

2. **Take Care of Yourself**   Do you get enough sleep and exercise? Do you eat a balanced diet? Try laughing often. It can actually stop disease.

3. **Stop Focusing on Your Problems**   It doesn't help to think about your problems and criticize yourself all the time. Instead, forget about yourself and help someone else. You'll feel better immediately.

4. **Don't Try to Control Everything**   You're not responsible for fixing everything that's wrong in the world. Let other people make mistakes. We all make them.

5. **Think Positively**   Remember that situations don't make us feel stress; our thinking does. Change your thinking. Imagine a happy ending, and then make it happen!

Answer the questions. Check *True* or *False*.

	True	False
1. Stress can be controlled.	_____	_____
2. Worrying can help you.	_____	_____
3. Helping other people is nice, but it's stressful.	_____	_____
4. It helps to keep as busy as possible.	_____	_____
5. Laughing can help stop stress.	_____	_____

UNIT 5

CITIZENSHIP AND DOCUMENTATION FOR WORK

OVERVIEW

Objectives

Skills and Structures

Talk about people's problems

Understand conversations

Understand citizenship requirements

Read an article

Understand line graphs, pie charts

Solve problems through writing

Brainstorm and write an article

Use modals of advice and necessity

Use short answers

Use tag endings

SCANS Competencies

Acquire and evaluate information: Student Book, Sound Bites, page 50; Student Book, Sound Bites, page 55; Student Book, Reading for Real, page 53; Workbook, Read, Think, and Write, page 29

Socialize: Student Book, Spotlight on Tag Endings, page 57

Participate as a team member and negotiate: Teacher's Manual, p. 83 Notes on Culture Corner

Realia

Forms, notices, and sample reading materials about citizenship

The 100 Questions or dictation sentences issued by INS

Possible visit by a citizenship instructor or advocate

Symbols of citizenship—the United States flag, a tape of the national anthem, and photocopies of the lyrics for the Star Spangled Banner

ACTIVITY NOTES

Page 49

Scene I

Preparation

1. Survey your students. Ask, "Do you know anyone who is a citizen? Who is interested in becoming a citizen? Who isn't sure?"

2. Next, generate a list of questions about citizenship. For example: "Who can apply? Where do I apply?" Students who are citizens, if there are any, can share their experiences in taking the citizenship test, and tell how citizenship changed their lives.

Sound Bites

While You Listen

Preparation

1. Write *apply, fill out, immigration, form, illegal,* and *fingerprint* on the board. Have students copy these words and any related words into their notebooks. Ask the class if they know what these words mean. Clarify as necessary. Have the students write the definitions or translations in their notebooks.

2. Have learners look at each illustration, read the situation, and guess what the advice might be in each case.

After You Listen

Extension

Part of the INS citizenship examination requires applicants to write one or more sentences from dictation. This is the section of the test most often failed. For this reason, give students practice in writing short sentences from dictation. Sentence dictation requires little time and can be done when there are a few minutes left in class. Here are some typical sentences from the INS citizenship exam.

- The President lives in the White House.
- There are fifty stars on the flag.
- The colors of the flag are red, white, and blue.

Listening Script

1. Stana: It says here that you have to be a permanent resident for five years before you can apply for citizenship.

   Maria: Yeah, so?

   Stana: Well, I've only been here three years, but I've heard that it takes so long to apply. Maybe I should start applying now.

   Maria: I think you should wait because they probably won't accept your application. You'll have to fill out all those forms again.

   Stana: Yeah, I guess you're right.

2. Han: I've lived in the United States for so long. Why should I become a citizen?

   Betsy: There are a lot of reasons.

   Han: Like what?

   Betsy: If you're a citizen, you can vote, and it may be easier for you to get certain jobs and benefits.

   Han: I didn't know that.

   Betsy: I think you should get some more information about citizenship.

3. Crispin: I'm afraid to take the test.

   Fred: Why?

   Crispin: It's so hard, and you have to speak a lot of English.

   Fred: Are you taking a citizenship class?

   Crispin: No.

   Fred: I think you ought to sign up for a class. You'll feel better.

4. Canan: I've really got some problems.

   Irene: What's the matter?

   Canan: A guy is going to help me fill out my immigration forms. He speaks my language.

   Irene: Yeah?

   Canan: But he wants $800 dollars. I can't pay that.

   Irene: That sounds illegal! I've got the number of the Immigrant Coalition downtown. I think you'd better call and get help.

   Canan: Thanks for telling me.

5. Linda: What's that?

   Jaime: They're my fingerprints. The INS didn't approve them!

   Linda: Let me see. It says here that you've got to get your fingerprints taken at one of these locations. You have to do them again.

   Jaime: I wish I knew that before.

6. Beatriz: I don't think I want to become a U.S. citizen.

   Inez: Why?

   Beatriz: I don't know. I don't want to forget my country.

   Inez: Maybe you don't have to. You should apply for dual citizenship.

   Beatriz: What's that?

   Inez: Sometimes you can be a citizen of both countries.

   Beatriz: That would be great.

Answers to Sound Bites

1. wait two years.
2. get some more information.
3. sign up for a class
4. call the Immigrant Coalition for help
5. get his fingerprints taken again.
6. apply for dual citizenship

Your Turn

Extension

Have learners think of additional advice to give each of the six characters. For example, "Han should talk to some U. S. citizens to get more information."

 Option 1: Have learners work in pairs to make a list of additional advice for each character in Sound Bites.

Option 2: Have the learners work in pairs or small groups and add on to the conversations in Sound Bites with the additional advice for each character. (You may want to make a copy of the listening script for the learners to refer to.) Have them present their conversations to the class.

Option 3: Have learners work in groups to brainstorm additional problems or questions a person might have about citizenship. Have them create dialogues where one person has the problem and the other offers advice. Have them present their conversations to the class.

Page 51

Spotlight on Modals of Advice and Necessity

Preparation

1. Introduce modals of advice and necessity either by distributing large strips of paper with the sentences written below or by reading aloud. Have the students head two columns on a sheet of paper with *Advice* or *Necessity*. Have students place each sentence under the appropriate heading.

   • You must have an ID card.
   • You've got to make an appointment first.
   • You should take a break.
   • You have to fill out this form.
   • You'd better try again.
   • You ought to get some help.

2. Let the students compare their answers with a partner. Clarify if necessary.

Answers to Exercise 1

1. e   2. f   3. a   4. b   5. d   6. c

Workbook

Workbook page 25 can be assigned after students have completed Student Book page 51.

Page 52

Person to Person

Extension

Have small groups of students practice modals of necessity by explaining rules they have heard (safety rules in the workplace, rules of driving, and so forth). Have the groups read their rules aloud and have the class guess the context.

Answers to Person to Person

Answers may vary. Some possible answers include:

That's too bad. We'll have to go without you.

Oh, no! You'd better get a job where you don't have to work weekends.

Page 53

Reading for Real

Preparation

Lead a discussion about naturalization. Make sure the learners understand what this means. Ask learners the following questions:

- Can a foreigner become a citizen of students' native country?
- What are the requirements for citizenship in their native country?
- What are the rules for naturalization in the United States?
- Can anyone become a citizen?
- What would be some benefits of becoming a citizen of another country?
- What might be the disadvantages of becoming a citizen of another country?

Exercise 2

Extension

1. The following suggestions can enhance students' understanding of U.S. history and government. Bring in forms, notices, and sample reading materials about citizenship. Provide students with up-to-date information, because rules and procedures are constantly changing.

2. Have a citizenship instructor or advocate conduct a question-and-answer session in your class. Bring in symbols of citizenship (for example, the United States flag with a cassette tape of the national anthem and copies of the Star Spangled Banner) to bring the material to life and spark discussion of U.S. history. Compare the U.S. flag and anthem with those of other countries.

Answers to Exercise 2

1. false   2. true   3. true   4. true   5. false

Page 54

Culture Corner

Preparation

Have learners look at the illustration, read the title, and guess what the article will be about. Make sure the students know that *INS* stands for Immigration and Naturalization Service and that its the part of the government that controls immigration. Ask, "How could INS rules separate a married couple?" Ask learners to relate any experiences they have had relating to this topic.

Exercise 3

Extension

Have students split into three groups for a mock trial or pretend court of justice. Group 1 represents Evelyn and Jonathan, Group 2 represents the INS, and Group 3 represents the jury (group of citizens who will decide the case). Groups 1 and 2 should prepare and argue their case. Group 3 should listen, discuss the arguments, and deliver a verdict (make a decision).

Answers to Exercise 3

Evelyn was too poor to sponsor someone for permanent residence. In addition, Jonathan had already created debt in the United States that he couldn't pay which also is against INS rules.

Page 55

Scene 2

Preparation

1. Quickly review the story line from Scene 1: Monique DuValle is waiting for her INS exam. She is trying to remember the answers to the 100 questions. She is very nervous. Note: As of the date this Teacher's Manual was published, citizenship applicants take a 10-item, written multiple-choice test based on the 100 questions about United States history and government. The written test is graded immediately. If applicants pass, they go directly to the oral interview, which is based on personal information from the N-400 form.

2. Ask students questions to find out what they already know about the procedures for naturalization.

Sound Bites

While You Listen

Preparation

1. Lead a discussion about people who have come to the country illegally. Ask the following questions:

   - How do the people get into the United States?
   - Why do they want to come?
   - How were they caught and what happened to them?
   - Do people try to live in students' native countries illegally?
   - What happens to them if they get caught?

2. Write *raid, to have papers, deported,* and *fine* (as financial penalty) on the board. Have students copy these words and any related words into their notebooks. Ask the class if they know what these words mean. Clarify if necessary. Have the students write the definitions or translations in their notebooks.

After You Listen

Presentation

After students listen and answer the questions, have them compare their answers with a partner.

Extension

Have an immigration lawyer or advocate give a talk in your class on changes in immigration law, immigrants' rights, discrimination, or related topics.

Listening Script

Yvonne: Hey, you just passed your citizenship test, didn't you?

Monique: Yes, I did

Yvonne: Congratulations!

Monique: Thanks . . . some people aren't so lucky.

Yvonne: Like who?

Monique: Did you hear about the raid over at the plant?

Yvonne: No, I didn't. What do you mean "raid"?

Monique: Immigration came in and arrested 100 workers.

Yvonne: Were they here illegally?

Monique: Yes, they were. No one had papers, or if they did, they were false. My friend Philippe was one of them.

Yvonne: Are they going to be deported?

Monique: Yeah, I think they are.

Yvonne: Will Immigration do anything to the company?

Monique: They probably won't. Or maybe they'll fine them.

Yvonne: What do you mean?

Monique: They might have to pay some money.

Yvonne: Hmm . . .

Monique: I'm glad I don't have to worry about myself anymore. But I can't stop thinking about Philippe.

Answers to Sound Bites

Answers may vary. Some possible answers: There was an immigration raid at the plant. One hundred workers were arrested. Philippe was arrested with the others, and they may be deported. The company may be fined.

Page 56

Spotlight on Short Answers

Preparation

1. Introduce short answers by asking individual students yes/no questions about personal data such as the following. "Are you from Ecuador? Is your last name Beric? Do you live in Elmhurst?" Let students know that you want more than yes or no answers. For example, "Yes, I am from Ecuador."

2. Make an overhead transparency of a personal data form that one of your students has filled out. Ask the class to answer questions such as "Is Neriman single? Does she have a job?" and so on.

Exercise 4

Extension

1. Think of other ways to elicit a variety of short answers with different auxiliaries. Try playing an abbreviated kind of Twenty Questions. Think of a well-known international person—for example, the President of the United States. Have students ask yes/no questions such as, "Is this person a woman? Is he living? Does he play sports?" and so on. You provide short answers. The player who guesses the mystery person wins (limit: 20 questions).

2. After a few games, let a student think of a specific person and answer the questions that the class asks. Eventually, break into small groups to play the game.

3. You may want to provide a list of famous international people for students to draw from, such as England's Queen Elizabeth, the Brazilian soccer player Pele, and so on.

Answers to Exercise 4

1. Yes, it is.
2. Yes, I was.
3. Yes, it is.
4. Yes, I am.
5. Yes, I can.
6. No, I'm not.

Your Turn

 Option 1: Have less advanced learners make the personalized substitutions using the dialogue in Exercise 4 as a model.

Option 2: Have the students work in pairs to create additional dialogues using other information from Monique's application for naturalization in Exercise 4. Have the partners present their dialogues to the class.

Option 3: Bring in copies of other forms that a person has to fill out to be naturalized. Have the students work in pairs to create dialogues using information from these forms.

Workbook

Workbook page 26 can be assigned after students have completed Student Book page 56.

Page 57

Spotlight on Tag Endings

Preparation

1. To introduce tag endings, begin again with questions about student-based personal data, such as "You're from Ecuador, aren't you? Your last name is Beric, isn't it? You live in Elmhurst, don't you?" Pause between questions and let students supply the tag ending. Try to elicit the rule—that if the auxiliary verb in the question is positive, the tag is negative; if the auxiliary is negative, the tag is positive.

2. Explain that people use tag endings when they think they know the answer but they want to be sure. This is why tag endings often make for excellent small talk (talking to be sociable, not for real information gathering).

Answers to Exercise 5

1. aren't we   2. isn't it   3. can we   4. isn't there   5. is it   6. do we

Answers to Exercise 6

1. weren't you   was
2. aren't you   answer will vary.
3. isn't it   answer will vary.
4. didn't you   answer will vary.

Workbook

Workbook pages 27 and 28 can be assigned after students have completed Student Book page 57.

Activity Masters

Activity Master 5-1 can be assigned after students have completed page 57.

Presentation

1. Demonstrate the activity by asking each student the first question, "Are you married?" Students should use short answers. On the board, tally their answers under *Yes* and *No*. (Many students will not be familiar with the tally system of four marks and a crossmark to indicate five.)

2. Cut out the questions before class and distribute one to each student. (For a smaller group of students, decide which questions to eliminate; for example, the ones referring to continents which are not represented in the class).

3. Ask students to circulate and ask the same question of everyone in the class. Have them tally the answers. Everyone's tally marks should total the same number (the number of students in the class, minus one). If necessary, put some model questions and short answers on the board for the students' reference during the activity.

4. Make an overhead transparency of the entire question list and record totals as the students call them out or record on the board. Talk about the trends in the class. For example, "Half of us have cars; only one of us has been in a car accident."

5. During the next class period practice tag endings by having students circulate again with their original questions and try to confirm what they remember each student told them. For example, "You have a job, don't you?" (Or, "You don't have a job, do you?") Again, students will use short answers to confirm or contradict.

Page 58

Get Graphic

Preparation

Lead a discussion about undocumented immigrants (illegal aliens) in the United States to find out what learners know about them. Ask the following questions:

- Are the numbers of undocumented people increasing or decreasing?
- Where do most undocumented people go in the United States?
- How do they enter the country?

Answers to Exercise 7

1. e   2. c   3. a   4. d   5. b

Answers to Exercise 8

1. true   2. true   3. false   4. false

Workbook

Workbook pages 29 and 30 can be assigned after students have completed Student Book page 58.

Activity Masters

Activity Master 5-2 can be assigned after students have completed page 58.

Presentation

1. Have the students study the information in the chart. Then have them read the directions and each statement and decide if the statement is true or false according to the information in the chart.

2. Have the students check their answers in pairs or as a class.

Page 59

Issues and Answers

Preparation

1. Find out who in the class has used a computer. Lead a discussion about the Worldwide Web, the Internet, and e-mail. Have learners look quickly at the e-mail message and ask the following questions:

   - What is this? Is it a standard letter?

   - Has anyone ever used the Internet and/or e-mail at work or at home?

   - Do you think the Internet and e-mail are useful tools in today's society? Why?

   - How can the Internet benefit your life?

Exercise 9

Extension

Have students find out how to get access to computers, the Internet, and e-mail—through school, work, or the public library.

Answers to Exercise 9

Answers may vary. Some possible answers are:

You can find the last name because the name given in the first message is the first letter of the first name combined with the last name (the total up to eight letters). Inga's last name is Sleb. Lisa's last name is Kent.

Inga is e-mailing from a company. The extension is *inc*.

Lisa is e-mailing from a school. The extension is *edu*.

They met when Inga was in Lisa's English class.

Inga needs to decide if she should become a citizen.

She is unsure.

Page 60

Wrap-Up

Presentation

If possible, involve students in the production of an immigrant student newsletter. If computers are available, have students type their paragraphs and add graphics. Use the newsletter as a reading text and note any grammatical errors for a future language-structure focus in class.

ANSWERS TO PROGRESS CHECKS

Progress Check A

Speak or Write

Answers will vary. Some possible answers are:

1. Monique is at the INS. She is waiting to take her citizenship exam.

2. She is nervous because she's not sure she can remember all the answers to the test. She's also afraid that she can't speak English well enough.

3. The examiner wants to know if Monique is telling the truth. Monique is promising to tell the truth.

4. Monique is thinking about Philippe because she's worried about him. He doesn't have papers, and she's not sure what's going to happen to him.

Listening Script

Undocumented people have some rights in the United States. If you are undocumented and you are arrested by the police, you have the right to contact a lawyer. You may also remain silent. You do not have to speak. You can wait until your lawyer is there to represent you.

Everyone has certain rights in the workplace. Everyone is entitled to a clean, safe workplace. For example, the floors should be clean so that you will not slip and have an accident. The air should not be unhealthy to breathe. If you work with dangerous chemicals or materials, you should have proper safety equipment and training to protect you.

Everyone should be paid at least minimum wage. You also have the right to join a union. Know your rights!

Listen

1. No   2. Yes   3. No   4. No   5. Yes

Progress Check B

Language Structures

A. 1. have to   2. should   3. don't have to   4. Shouldn't

B. 1. am   2. I don't   3. didn't you   4. have you

Content

1. permanent resident   2. petition   3. oath   4. INS   5. barred   6. raid

ANSWERS TO ACTIVITY MASTERS

Activity Master 5-1

Answers will vary.

Activity Master 5-2

1. False   2. True   3. True   4. False   5. True

REPRODUCIBLE MASTER
Unit 5

WORKBOOK ANSWERS

Practice 1
Answers may vary. Some possible answers are:

1. ought to/should
2. have to/need to
3. have to/should/must
4. have to
5. have to/must

Practice 5
1. c 2. e 3. a 4. b 5. d

Practice 6
1. This is your passport, isn't it?

2. You need a visa now, don't you?

3. There are three branches of government, aren't there?

4. The President appointed those judges, didn't he *or* she?

5. The citizenship interview was difficult, wasn't it?

Practice 7
1. should/ought to
2. should/ought to/must
3. ought to/should
4. has to/should
5. should/ought to

Practice 8
Executive Branch: enforces laws; President, Vice President, and
 Cabinet (advisors); White House; President's term is four years.

Judicial Branch: interprets laws; nine Supreme Court justices;
 Supreme Court in Washington, D.C.; life terms

Senate: makes laws; 100 Senators—two from each of the 50 states;
 Capitol Building; six-year terms

House of Representatives: makes laws; 435 representatives
 (congressmen and -women). The number of congressmen from
 each state depends on that state's population; two-year terms

REPRODUCIBLE MASTER
UNIT 5

PROGRESS CHECK A

SPEAK OR WRITE

Look at the pictures from Unit 5. Use the questions below to talk or write about each picture. Retell the story in your own words.

Questions
1. Where is Monique, and why is she there?
2. Why does she seem nervous?
3. Why is the examiner asking Monique this question?
4. Why is Monique thinking about Philippe?

LISTEN

While you listen, check the correct answer.

	Yes	No
1. If you are arrested, you must speak to the police.	_____	_____
2. You can ask a lawyer to represent you.	_____	_____
3. The place where you work must be clean and attractive.	_____	_____
4. Your employers may provide safety equipment, but they don't have to.	_____	_____
5. Undocumented people can join a union.	_____	_____

REPRODUCIBLE MASTER

UNIT 5   PROGRESS CHECK B

LANGUAGE STRUCTURES

Complete the sentences with *should, shouldn't, have to,* or *don't have to.*

1. To become a citizen, you _____ take a test.

2. You _____ ask a friend to practice the questions with you. That way, you'll feel more prepared.

3. If you're over 50 and you've lived as a permanent resident for 20 years, you _____ take the written test.

4. _____ you be leaving now? The test starts in one hour!

Use the correct short answer or tag ending.

1. Are you going to take the citizenship test?

   Yes, I _____.

2. Do you feel nervous?

   No, _____.

3. You took a citizenship class, _____?

4. You haven't taken the test before, _____?

CONTENT

Look at the words in the box. Complete the sentences below with the correct word(s).

raid	oath	permanent resident
petition	INS	barred

To become a citizen, you must be a (1) _____. You must also fill out a (2) _____ for naturalization. You will have to take an (3) _____, which is a promise to the United States. The (4) _____ can approve or reject your application. If you ran away from the United States Army, you are (5) _____ from citizenship; you can never apply for it. Living without documentation can be risky. If there is a (6) _____ at the company where you work, you can be deported.

© NTC/Contemporary Publishing Group, Inc.

Name _____ Date _____

ACTIVITY MASTER 5-1

CLASS SURVEY WITH SHORT ANSWERS AND TAG ENDINGS

See Teacher's Manual page 87 for complete directions on this activity.

1. Are you married? — Yes No

2. Do you have children? — Yes No

3. Do you have family members living in the United States? — Yes No

4. Are you from Central or South America? — Yes No

5. Are you from Europe? — Yes No

6. Are you from Africa? — Yes No

7. Are you from Asia? — Yes No

8. Do you have a car? — Yes No

9. Have you ever been in a car accident? — Yes No

10. Do you have a job? — Yes No

11. Do you have health insurance? — Yes No

12. Do you smoke cigarettes? — Yes No

13. Are you a United States citizen? — Yes No

14. Have you ever voted in an election in any country? — Yes No

15. Do you read any newspapers? — Yes No

16. Do you have a computer at home? — Yes No

17. Have you ever used the Internet? — Yes No

18. Have you ever visited a home in the United States? — Yes No

19. Are you happy living in the United States? — Yes No

20. Do you plan to go back to your native country to live? — Yes No

Name _____ Date _____

MORE GRAPHIC SKILLS: RIGHTS OF UNITED STATES CITIZENS

Rights	Undocumented Person	Permanent Resident	Citizen
Right to vote	No	No	Yes
Cannot be deported	No	No	Yes
Right to be elected	No	No	Yes
Right to travel and re-enter the United States	No	Limited	Yes
Right to petition to bring in family members	No	Limited	Yes
Right to work	No	Limited	Yes
Protected by the Bill of Rights	Limited	Limited	Yes
Right to own land	Limited	Limited	Yes
Right to social security benefits	No	Limited	Yes
Right to serve on a jury	No	No	Yes
Right to carry a United States passport	No	No	Yes
Right to United States diplomatic protection	No	No	Yes

Answer the questions. Check *True* or *False*.

	True	False
1. Undocumented people have no rights.	_____	_____
2. Permanent residents may get some social security benefits.	_____	_____
3. Undocumented people cannot work.	_____	_____
4. Undocumented people can visit their country and return to the United States.	_____	_____
5. Permanent residents can be deported.	_____	_____

UNIT 6 ENTERTAINMENT AND THE ARTS

OVERVIEW

Objectives

Skills and Structures

Talk about people's problems

Understand conversations about socializing at work

Read a performance brochure

Talk about dancing

Make a bar graph

Read and solve problems

Use an idea map

Use present participles as adjectives

Use past participles as adjectives

Choose the correct adjective

SCANS Competencies

See things in the mind's eye: Student Book, Sound Bites, page 62

Make decisions: Student Book, Talk About It, page 65

Teach others: Student Book, Culture Corner, page 66

Realia

Entertainment section of newspaper

Instructional dance video

Brochure or flyers from local arts groups

TV listings

Memos or flyers from workplace about social events

ACTIVITY NOTES

Page 61

Scene 1

Preparation

Ask students the following questions and write their responses on the board:

- What is entertainment?
- What things do you for entertainment?
- What are "the arts"?
- What things do you do that involve "the arts"?

Presentation

After learners retell the story, divide the class into groups. Give each group an entertainment/arts section from the newspaper. Have each group use the newspaper to make a lists of entertainment and arts activities. Have learners circle items that are new (not the ones put on the board in the first activity).

Extension

Have pairs of students role-play the Scene in one of several ways. Bring in props or costumes to make the activity more interesting. If possible, videotape the role plays and have students critique their own performances.

 Option 1: Students can perform the lines as written. You can assign pairs or let students choose their own partners.

Option 2: Students can make a simple substitution in some lines (by having Victoria sing or paint, for example).

Option 3: More advanced students can imagine they saw Victoria's injury and are talking about what happened.

Page 62

Sound Bites

Preparation

With the class discuss what kind of things students usually discuss with co-workers besides work. Write student ideas on the board. Leave them there while students listen to the Sound Bites. Did any of the co-workers talk about similar things?

Presentation

Before playing the tape, have students read the sentences and look at the pictures in the chart. Answer any questions.

Listening Script

1. Lydia: Hi Kathryn. Did you have a nice weekend?

   Kathryn: I sure did. My husband and I went to the international dance program at the community college.

   Lydia: How was it?

   Kathryn: There were some really fascinating dances. The costumes and the music were great too.

   Lydia: What did you like the best?

   Kathryn: Oh, the Spanish gypsy dances. I love to watch flamenco dancers.

2. Jan: So what did you do last weekend, Mark?

   Mark: Not much. How about you?

   Jan: I watched the soccer game between Mexico and El Salvador on Sunday. Didn't you?

   Mark: Yeah, I did. What did you think of the game?

   Jan: I thought it was pretty boring until the last 10 minutes. Wow! Three goals in a row.

3. Barb: Julie, you like classical music, don't you?

   Julie: I love it. That's all I listen to.

   Barb: Well, would you like to go to a concert? A group of us from work are going in November.

Julie:	When? Where? How much is it?
Barb:	November 8th at the Prairie Center for the Performing Arts. The tickets are $30.00 a piece.
Julie:	OK. It sounds like an interesting way to spend a Saturday night.
4. Anthony:	Tom, you like science fiction, right?
Tom:	Uh huh. Why?
Anthony:	Well, have you seen the movie, *Starship Soldiers?*
Tom:	Yeah.
Anthony:	Did you like it? My girlfriend wants to see it on Friday night.
Tom:	Don't waste your money. The story was confusing, and the acting was terrible.

Answers to Sound Bites

1. The event was an international dance program. It was on the weekend. There were fascinating dances.
2. The event was a soccer game. It was last weekend. The game was boring.
3. The event is a concert. It will be on November 8. It sounds interesting.
4. The event is a science-fiction movie. It is on Friday. The story is confusing.

Page 63

Spotlight on Present Participles as Adjectives

Presentation

After students have read the example sentences in the Spotlight Box, have them write new sentences in their notebook with the adjectives in the examples. Ask volunteers to write their sentences on the board.

Answers to Exercise 1

Answers will vary. Here are some possible answers:

1. entertaining	2. amazing	3. boring	4. confusing
5. frustrating	6. embarrassing	7. disappointing	8. annoying
9. exhausting	10. entertaining		

Page 64

Person to Person

Preparation

Have students read through the conversations individually, and underline the present participles as adjectives. Review the meanings with the class.

Workbook

Workbook page 31 can be assigned after students have completed Student Book page 64.

Reading for Real

Extension

Divide the class into groups of three. Give each group a different entertainment ad from the newspaper (plays, concerts, movies, and so on.) Have each group write three to five questions about the ad. Have the groups exchange ads and answer the questions. Here are some example questions:

- What is the title or name of the event?
- Where is it?
- When is it?
- How much does it cost?

Answers to Exercise 2

1. false   2. false   3. true   4. true   5. false

Culture Corner

Preparation

In small groups have students talk about dancing in their native country. Ask questions such as the following:

- Do people dance often or only on special occasions?
- Does everyone dance?
- What are some popular dances?
- Is there special music?

Extension

Bring in a "how to" dance video for the class to watch and follow the directions. Most video rental stores, such as Blockbuster or Hollywood Video, have such videos. If you can't find a how-to video, show a dance video of one of the dances in the list in Culture Corner, and ask the following questions:

- Do you like this dance?
- Can you do it?
- Would you like to learn how to do it? Explain.

Exercise 3

Preparation

Have students guess the country or region most closely associated with each dance. If any students cannot guess, provide them with the following answers: ballet (France), belly dancing (Middle East), bharata natya (India), country-western line dancing (U.S.), flamenco (Spain), Kabuki (Japan), mambo (Latin America), mazurka (Poland), polka (Germany), salsa (Mexico), square dancing (U.S.), tango (Argentina), tap dancing (U.S.)

Scene 2

Preparation

In small groups have students discuss what they planned to do with their lives when they were younger. Poll the class to see how many students have changed their plans.

Sound Bites

Preparation

With the class discuss the dynamics of family arguments in students' native countries. Are children or young adults allowed to argue with their parents? Does every family member contribute to the decision, or are decisions made by only one person? How is this different from the way family arguments are resolved in the United States?

Presentation

Before playing the tape, read through the questions with the class. Clarify any words students are unfamiliar with.

Extension

Bring in continuing-education flyers or brochures from your community. Divide learners into groups. Give each group a brochure and ask them to locate classes that relate to entertainment or the arts. Have each group select classes of interest to them. Then have groups interview each other about the classes they selected. Some questions the groups might ask each other include the following:

- What is the class?
- When is it?
- Where is it?
- How much does it cost?
- Why did you select this class?

Listening Script

Victoria:	No, Dad. I don't want to quit dancing. My leg will heal, and I can go back to work.
Pablo:	That's not the point. I'm worried about you. You have a broken leg now, but what will happen next?
Victoria:	Nothing. I was tired, and I fell. It was just a stupid accident.
Pablo:	No, it wasn't. You were dancing eight hours a day, and you were exhausted. That will happen again and again.
Victoria:	You can't see into the future!
Pablo:	Yes I can. I see an injured dancer with no future. You must go to college. Get an education. Then, if you can't dance, you can do something else.
Victoria:	I want to dance. I don't want to do anything else.

Pablo:	I understand that. But you need more. Learn how to teach others to dance. Learn how to run a business. Maybe you can open your own dance school some day.
Victoria:	I don't want to talk about this anymore. I'm so irritated I want to scream.

Answers to Sound Bites

1. Victoria doesn't want to quit dancing.

2. Her father is worried because Victoria has a broken leg.

3. If she continues her education, she can learn how to teach dancing, run a business, or open her own dance school.

Page 68

Spotlight on Past Participles as Adjectives

Presentation

After students have read through the examples in the Spotlight Box, have them turn to the appendix. With a partner, have them scan the past participles and write down an example of each type of past-participial ending in their notebooks, with an example for future reference.

Answers to Exercise 4

1. worried (I)
2. broken (leg)
3. tired (I)

4. exhausted (you)
5. uneducated (dancer)
6. frustrated (I)

Workbook

Workbook page 32 can be assigned after students have completed Student Book page 68.

Page 69

Spotlight on Participles as Adjectives

Presentation

After students have read the example sentences in the Spotlight Box, have them try to write their own sentence pairs using adjectives such as *confused/confusing*, *tired/tiring*, or *surprising/surprised*. Ask volunteers to write their sentence pairs on the board.

Extension

Have learners bring in memos or announcements from their workplaces about social events. OR create your own memo or announcement. Make copies and transparencies of the announcements. Have learners scan the announcements for specific information. Ask learners to write questions to ask each other about the memos or announcements.

Exercise 5

Extension

Have learners work with a partner. Ask them to draw a line from the participial adjective in each sentence to the noun it modifies. Ask for volunteers to write each sentence on the board.

Answers to Exercise 5

1. interesting
2. surprising
3. irritated
4. shocked
5. confusing
6. fascinating
7. disappointing
8. tired

Workbook

Workbook pages 33 and 34 can be assigned after students have completed Student Book page 69.

Activity Masters

Activity Master 6-1 may be assigned after learners have completed Student Book page 69.

Presentation

Monitor the learners' sentences while they play the game.

Extension

Have them write their sentences on paper. Collect the papers after the game. Make copies of the sentences for the learners. Have learners read the sentences and underline the participles used as adjectives in each one for homework.

Page 70

Get Graphic

Presentation

After students have read through the information in the graph, ask the following questions:

- How much total money did this family spend on entertainment last month?
- Do you think this was too much? Why or why not?

Activity Masters

Activity Master 6-2 may be assigned after learners have completed Student Book page 70.

Exercise 7

Presentation

You may wish to have students write and exchange the letters anonymously.

Workbook

Workbook pages 35 and 36 can be assigned after students have completed Student Book page 72.

ANSWERS FOR PROGRESS CHECKS

Progress Check A

Speak or Write

1. She broke her leg.

2. He wanted her to get an education (go to college). He wanted her to have more opportunities. He was afraid that she would be injured again and would have nothing to do if she couldn't dance.

3. She obeyed her father. She went to college and graduated. Some possible reasons: She respected her father. She understood his reasons.

Listening Script

America's Dancing Ambassador Goes on Tour

The world-famous Ballet Folklórico de Mexico is touring the United States. Amalia Hernandez started the Ballet Folklórico in 1952. In 1997, she was 80 years old and still working with the dance company. Actually, there are two Ballet Folklórico dance companies. One stays in Mexico all year. The other is a touring company that travels around the world.

Amalia Hernandez started dancing when she was eight years old. She first became interested in dancing when her parents took her on vacations to small towns in Mexico. Later she saw Russian ballet dancers and took classical ballet lessons. Amalia dreamed of combining Mexican folk dances with ballet. She developed dozens of ballets that are inspired by dances from more than 60 regions in Mexico.

On this tour, audiences will see the performance of *Guelaguetza* (*way-law-wet-sa*) for the first time in the United States. *Guelaguetza* features dances from seven regions of the state of Oaxaca (*wa-ha-ka*). Men perform the feather dance from the Zapoteca region. Women perform a dance from the Mixteca culture.

Hernandez also started the Children's Cultural Education Fund in 1991. The project introduces more than 30,000 children in the United States to the Ballet Folklórico de Mexico. It gives free performances and also provides classroom materials.

Hernandez's two daughters are also interested in dancing. One daughter is a dancer, and the other trains dancers.

According to Amalia Hernandez, "Dance is a language that everybody understands."

Listen

1. b   2. a   3. a   4. c

Progress Check B

Language Structures

1. interesting   4. amazed
2. injured   5. entertaining
3. fascinating

Content

1. b   2. c   3. a   4. c   5. b

ANSWERS TO ACTIVITY MASTERS

Activity Master 6-1

Sentences will vary.

Activity Master 6-2

Category	Value
News	22
Sports	16
Talk Shows	6
Movies	23
Sitcoms	10
Dramas	4
Soap Operas	14
Educational Programs	5
Game Shows	9

5   10   15   20   25

UNIT 6
WORKBOOK ANSWERS

Practice 1
1. depressing   2. exciting   3. thrilling   4. annoying

Practice 3
1. The audience was shocked when the dancer fell down.

2. Elena's mom was worried when she did not call.

3. Robert was embarrassed when his car did not start.

4. Ed's grandmother was injured in a car accident.

5. She had a broken arm.

6. The young man looked interested when he heard about the beautiful actress.

7. The students were disappointed when the teacher was absent.

Practice 4
1. boring   6. confusing

2. bored   7. shocking

3. pleasing   8. shocked

4. pleased   9. interesting

5. confused   10. Interested

Practice 5
Answers may vary. Here are some possible answers:

1. thrilling 2. amazing 3. exhausted 4. confused 5. surprising   6. exciting

Practice 7
1. Amalia Hernandez started the Ballet Folklórico de Mexico in <u>1952</u>.

2. <u>One dance company</u> only performs in Mexico City.

3. <u>One touring group</u> travels around the world.

4. <u>She became interested in dancing</u> when she was on vacation.

5. It teaches <u>American</u> school children.

REPRODUCIBLE MASTER
UNIT 6

PROGRESS CHECK A

SPEAK OR WRITE

Look at these pictures from Unit 6. Use the questions below to talk
or write about each picture.

Questions

1. What happened to Victoria?

2. What did Victoria's father want her to do? Why?

3. What did Victoria do? Why?

LISTEN

While you listen, circle the correct answers.

1. The Ballet Folklórico de Mexico is known
   a. only in Mexico.   b. worldwide   c. only in the U. S.

2. The Ballet Folklórico combines ballet with
   a. Mexican folk dances   b. Russian dances   c. modern dances

3. Amalia Hernandez became interested in dancing when she was
   a. eight years old   b. eighteen years old   c. eighty years old

4. Amalia Hernandez is
   a. retired   b. semi-retired   c. still working

PROGRESS CHECK B

LANGUAGE STRUCTURES

Circle the correct adjective in each sentence.

1. Mike and Nancy saw an *interesting/interested* movie last night.

2. The movie was about an *injuring/injured* basketball player.

3. The basketball player had a *fascinating/fascinated* life.

4. Mike and Nancy were *amazing/amazed* by the story.

5. They told all their friends to see this *entertaining/entertained* movie.

CONTENT

Circle the correct answer.

1. Flamenco and ballet are kinds of

   a. sports.   b. dances.   c. movies.

2. Small talk can be conversation about

   a. important world events.
   b. personal family problems.
   c. weekend activities.

3. *Entertainment* means

   a. doing something for fun
   b. doing something for work
   c. doing something for school

4. Which of the following is not related to the arts?

   a. going to a play
   b. going to a museum
   c. going to a wedding

5. Which sentence is true about talking with co-workers in the United States?

   a. People never talk to co-workers.
   b. Co-workers often talk to one another.
   c. Employers don't want their employees to talk to one another.

REPRODUCIBLE MASTER

UNIT 6

ACTIVITY MASTER 6-1

BOARD GAME
ARE YOU BORED OR BORING?

Start	bored	annoyed	exhausting	interested
End				
interesting				boring
worried				fascinated
confusing				relaxing
amazed				irritated
thrilling				exciting
excited				surprised
disappointing	embarrassed	entertaining	tired	frustrating

- Work in a groups of 2–4.

- Give each person a different marker.

- Have the person with the first birthday of the year start the game.

- Flip a coin. Tails moves one place. Heads moves two places.

- Use the word you land on correctly in a sentence. Everyone in the group writes the sentences on a piece of paper.

- Check with your teacher if you are not sure the sentence is correct.

- The first person to move around the board wins.

MORE GRAPHIC SKILLS

Watching television is one of the most popular forms of
entertainment. Read about the kinds of programs students from one
English class watch in a week. Work with a partner and use the
information to fill in the bar graph below.

Kinds of Programs	Number of Watchers
News	22
Sports	16
Talk Shows	6
Movies	23
Sitcoms	10
Dramas	4
Soap Operas	14
Educational Programs	5
Game Shows	9

News

Sports

Talk Shows

Movies

Sitcoms

Dramas

Soap Operas

Educational
Programs

Game Shows

      5   10   15   20   25

Write four to six questions about the graph on another piece of
paper. Then exchange questions with another pair. One student
answers questions 1, 3, and 5. The other student answers questions
2, 4, and 6.

UNIT 7   OUR WATERS

OVERVIEW

Objectives

Skills and Structures

Talk about people's problems

Understand recorded conversations

Read a recipe

Read a map

Make a bar graph

Discuss ways to conserve water

Read and write letters to the editor

Make an idea map

Use relative clauses with *who*

Use relative clauses with *which* and *that*

Use correct word order in relative clauses

SCANS Competencies

Interpret and communicate information: Student Book, Sound Bites, page 74; Participate as member of a team: Student Book, Reading for Real page 77; Problem-solving: Student Book, Culture Corner, page 78

Realia

Magazine pictures from a variety of water sports and activities (white-water rafting and houseboats, for example)

Pictures of various fish (swordfish, bluefin tuna): check encyclopedias or the Internet for pictures if you can't find them in magazines.

Fish or seafood recipes

U.S. map

Map of your state

Letters to the editor from local newspapers

Poster board and markers

ACTIVITY NOTES

Page 73

Scene 1

Preparation

Ask learners to say the first word that comes to mind when they think of water. Write the words on the board as learners say them. Continue until learners can think of no more words. Discuss the words with the class. Have learners copy the words in their notebooks.

Extension

1. Refer learners to this list of words as they complete each page of the unit. Have them put a check next to each word or idea that appears in the unit.

2. Have pairs of students role-play the Scene in one of several ways. Bring in props or costumes to make the activity more interesting. If possible, videotape the role plays and have students critique their own performances.

Option 1: Students can perform the monologue as written, adding lines they write themselves.

Option 2: Students can make a simple substitution in some lines (by having Andrew do another job, for example).

Option 3: More advanced students can pretend they are fishermen with the same problem and tell the class how they feel.

Sound Bites

Preparation

In small groups have students brainstorm the kinds of questions reporters usually ask. Then tell them to list three or four specific questions they would like to ask Andrew.

While You Listen

Presentation

Before you play the tape or read the conversation, remind students to listen for the questions they wrote. Did the reporter ask all their questions?

After You Listen

Extension

After learners have answered the reporter's questions, read the script or play the listening tape again. Ask learners to write the parts of sentences they hear that begin with the word *who*. (There are four *who* clauses in the script that follows.)

On the board write the sentences in the order in which they appear. Have learners supply the *who* clauses. Underline the *who* clauses.

Explain that these clauses give more information about people. Ask learners to identify the people that the clauses give more information about.

Listening Script

Reporter:	Well, Mr. Lan, why don't you tell me a little about yourself before we start talking about the problems of the people who fish in these waters.
Mr. Lan:	Okay. What do you want to know?
Reporter:	First of all, how long have you been a fisherman?
Mr. Lan:	All my life. My father was a fisherman who had his own boat in Vietnam. When I came to the United States 25 years ago, fishing was all I could do. I didn't have to speak English to fish.
Reporter:	Have you always had your own boat?
Mr. Lan:	Oh, no. I just bought this boat a few years ago. First I worked for my uncle, who sponsored me when I came to the United States. My uncle's an old guy who retired about five years ago. When he did, I decided to buy his boat.

Reporter:	You must be pretty successful if you own your own boat.
Mr. Lan:	I was doing OK until last year. Now I don't know if I can keep my boat.
Reporter:	What's changed for you?
Mr. Lan:	This. Look at the diseased and deformed fish in those buckets over there.
Reporter:	What's causing this?
Mr. Lan:	I'm not sure, but I think the chicken farmers around here are dumping waste in the rivers.
Reporter:	What are you going to do?
Mr. Lan:	I don't know. Maybe I'll have to sell my boat.

Answers to Sound Bites

1. Andrew Lan has been a fisherman all his life.
2. He bought his boat from his uncle about five years ago.
3. Many of the fish he catches are diseased and deformed.
4. The chicken farmers may be dumping waste in the rivers.
5. He doesn't know what he is going to do. Maybe he'll have to sell his boat.

Page 75

Spotlight on Relative Clauses with *Who*

Presentation

After students have read the examples in the Spotlight Box, elicit that *who* clauses always follow the noun or pronoun they modify.

Exercise 1

Preparation

Have students discuss the sentences with a partner to clarify any unfamiliar vocabulary. If students are still unsure about some words, provide the definition and an example.

Answers to Exercise 1

1. Jack is a neighbor who owns a boat.
2. I have a friend named Janet who lives near a river.
3. You met my cousin who goes white-water rafting every summer.
4. This is my co-worker who likes to go fishing.
5. Meet my ESL teacher who swims a mile every day.

Workbook

Workbook page 37 can be assigned after students have completed Student Book page 75.

Person to Person

Preparation

1. Write the following words on the board:
   - white-water rafting
   - houseboat
   - swordfish

   Ask learners to define the words if they can. Show pictures of the words after learners have talked about them. Use pictures from magazines or encyclopedias.
2. Give learners copies of a map of the United States. Have them locate Wisconsin and the Mississippi River. Do a survey to find out who has been to each place.
3. Give learners copies of a map of the world. Have them locate the Atlantic Ocean and the Mediterranean Sea. Ask who has seen either of these.
4. Make a chart on the board that shows who has been to or seen Wisconsin, the Mississippi River, the Atlantic Ocean, and the Mediterranean Sea.
5. Have learners work with a partner to write sentences about the chart. Ask each pair to read one of its sentences to the rest of the class.

Extension

Have students present one of the conversations to the class in one of several ways.

 Option 1: Students can add lines to the existing conversations.

Option 2: Students can pretend they are in the conversations and present their own opinions about what the characters did.

Reading for Real

Preparation

1. Have students read the first paragraph silently. Have learners take out their maps from page 76 and ask them to locate the following places:
   - the states that make up the Pacific Northwest
   - the Mississippi River
   - Maryland and Virginia
2. Have a brief class discussion about regional food and seafood. Ask learners to share information with the class about special foods that are featured in different parts of their native countries.

Presentation

Have students underline any unfamiliar vocabulary as they read. Review the meaning of these words as a class.

Exercise 2

Extension

Call out words or phrases from the recipes and have students underline or circle them. Explain that the purpose is to read as quickly as possible to find the answers.

Answers for Exercise 2

1. Takes several hours to cook—neither
2. Is low in fat—salmon
3. Serves four—salmon
4. Cooks in the broiler—salmon
5. Contains fresh fruit—neither

Activity Masters

Activity Master 7-1 can be assigned after learners have completed Student Book page 77.

Page 78

Culture Corner

Preparation

In small groups have students discuss the picture. Ask learners the following questions:

- What do you see in the river?
- What do the signs say?
- Have you ever seen anything like this before in the United States?
- Have you ever seen anything like this in your home country?

Presentation

Depending on the level of your students, you may want to read the paragraph sentence by sentence to explain and clarify the ideas.

Answers to In Your Experience

1. Lake Erie
2. Lake Huron
3. Lake Ontario
4. Lake Michigan
5. Lake Superior
6. Ohio River
7. Mississippi River
8. Missouri River
9. Atlantic Ocean
10. Pacific Ocean
11. Gulf of Mexico

Page 79

Scene 2

Preparation

Read the text line above the comic strips. In small groups have students discuss what they would do if they were forced to stop doing a job they really enjoyed. Some students may have had this experience when they came to the United States.

Sound Bites

While You Listen

Presentation

Play the tape of the conversation or read it to the class.

After You Listen

Extension

1. Have learners work with a partner or in a small group. Ask them to make a list of all of the skills they think a fisherman has. Have them decide what kind of job Andrew should look for.

2. Debrief by asking the reporter from each group to share with the class.

Listening Script

Lukas:	Andrew, what kind of job are you interested in?
Andrew:	I don't know for sure yet. I had a job that I loved. I hope I can find another job that I like as much.
Lukas:	Tell me a little about the work that you did.
Andrew:	I've been a fisherman all my life. About five years ago, I bought my own boat, which I recently had to sell. I couldn't catch enough fish to pay for the loan for the boat, feed my family, and pay my other bills!
Lukas:	Do you have any education or special skills that you want to tell me about?
Andrew:	I graduated from high school, and I've taken a few community college classes in subjects that interested me.
Lukas:	Oh, like what?
Andrew:	I took classes in biology, small-business management, and accounting . . . things that helped me to do my job better.
Lukas:	Why aren't you a fisherman anymore?
Andrew:	Haven't you heard about all the fish that died in the waters around here? I couldn't catch enough healthy fish to sell. A lot of us who had just one or two boats couldn't make a living anymore. We couldn't compete against the big companies that own huge boats.

Answers to Sound Bites

Andrew doesn't know what kind of job he is interested in.

He isn't a fisherman anymore because he had to sell his boat. He couldn't catch enough fish to pay his bills and support his family.

Spotlight on Relative Clauses with *Which* and *That*

Presentation

After students have read the example sentences in the Spotlight Box, again emphasize that the clause beginning with *which* or *that* follows the noun or pronoun it modifies.

Exercise 3

Extension

Have pairs perform all or part of the dialogue in front of the class.

Answers to Exercise 3

The following words should be circled; the following phrases underlined

job; that I loved

job; that I like as much

work; that you did

boat; which I recently had to sell

education or skills; that you wanted to tell me about

subjects; that interested me

things; that also helped me do my job better

fish; that died in the waters around here

us; who had just one or two boats

Workbook

Workbook page 38 can be assigned after students have completed Student Book page 80.

Spotlight on Word Order in Relative Clauses

Presentation

After students have read the example sentences in the Spotlight Box, have them turn to page 83. They should underline all the clauses with *who, which,* or *that,* and count how many come in the middle of the sentence and how many come at the end.

Answers to Exercise 4

Answers will vary. Here are some possible answers:

1. Environmentalists who study fish and water believe there is a worldwide fish crisis.
2. Building and pollution are dangerous activities that kill fish.
3. Fishermen who catch bluefin tuna sell the tuna to Japan for as much as $80,000.
4. A fisherman who catches a bluefin tuna can make a lot of money.
5. Consumers who refuse to buy endangered fish can stop overfishing.

Workbook

Workbook pages 39 and 40 can be assigned after learners have completed Student Book page 81.

Activity Masters

Activity Master 7-2 may be assigned after learners have completed Student Book page 81. Scramble the beginnings and ends for the sentences before you give them to learners.

 Option: For less advanced learners, use this activity as a whole class match-up. Give learners beginnings or endings of sentences and ask them to find the match. Debrief by having each matched pair read their completed sentence to the rest of the class. Have the class decide if the sentences are correct or incorrect.

Page 82

Get Graphic

Preparation

Ask students to get out their world maps. Have them locate each country listed in the table.

- Ask the following questions:
- Which countries are in Asia?
- Which countries are in Europe?
- Which countries are in South America?
- Which countries are in Africa?

Presentation

After students have finished reading the table, check comprehension by asking questions such as the following:

- Which country caught the least fish?
- Which Asian country caught the most fish?
- Which South American country caught the most fish?
- How many fish did the United States catch?

Answers to Exercise 5

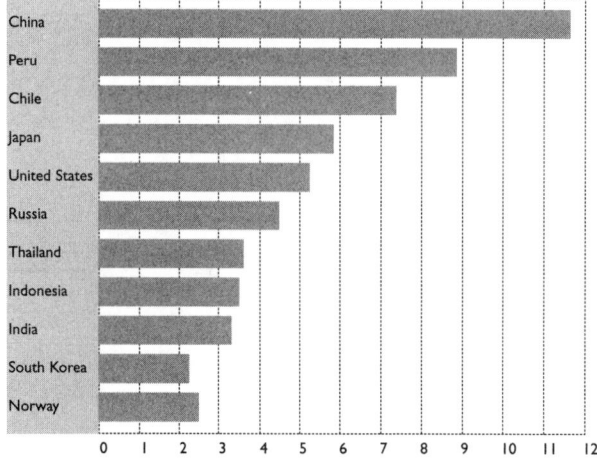

Answers to Exercise 6

Answers will vary. Here are some possible answers:

1. A Vegetarian Reader: Fishermen are killers who deserve no sympathy.

2. Sue Nickols: Pollution is the problem, and Andrew Lan is not a fish killer.

Wrap-Up

Presentation

Remind students to think about how to protect waters around the world, not just in the United States.

Workbook

Workbook pages 41 and 42 may be assigned after learners have completed page 84.

ANSWERS FOR PROGRESS CHECKS

Progress Check A

Speak or Write

Answers will vary but may include the following:

1. He is a fisherman.

2. He doesn't catch enough healthy fish to sell.

3. He might train for other jobs or he might be unemployed.

Listening Script

The Mountain God and the River God

Once upon a time in Vietnam, there was a beautiful princess who was the king's only daughter. Both the mountain god and the river god wanted to marry her, so the king said, "You two will fight, and the god who wins will marry the princess."

The two gods fought and fought with their bows and arrows. At last, the mountain god won and got to marry the beautiful princess. But the river god was a poor loser who became very angry and attacked the mountain. The river got higher and higher and covered the mountain. It rose up to the top where the mountain god and the princess lived. The mountain got higher too, so the river god could not get the princess.

That happened many years ago. In Vietnam, there is a rainy season which is in July and August. And even today, when the rains come and the rivers rise, people say that the jealous river god is still trying to take away the princess.

Listen

1. False   2. True   3. False   4. True   5. False

Progress Check B

Language Structures

1. I have a new neighbor who is from St. Louis, Missouri.
2. Our houses, which are next door to each other, are on a lake.
3. Betty has three sons who are married.
4. Her oldest son owns a computer software business that is very successful.
5. Her youngest son, who lives in Maine, is a lobster fisherman.

Content

1. a   2. c   3. b   4. c   5. a

ANSWERS FOR ACTIVITY MASTERS

Activity Master 7-1

1. True   2. False   3. False   4. False   5. False

Student sentences will vary.

Activity Master 7-2

Student sentences will vary.

The master contains the following sentences:

I have a friend who works three jobs.

We found a house that we want to buy.

She has a job that she hates.

He has a boss that he likes a lot.

I bought a book that was on the best seller list.

We moved to neighborhood which has many parks.

That's my uncle who is a pilot.

Our city has a mayor who is concerned about water pollution.

Do you know which VCR you want to buy?

I use a computer which is easy to operate.

REPRODUCIBLE MASTER
UNIT 7

WORKBOOK ANSWERS

Practice 1

1. Robert has three cousins who live in Vietnam and are fishermen.

2. Rosa talked to two people who are going to the Caribbean on a cruise.

3. My friends met a man who is starting his own company.

4. Eva had dinner with a friend who is a job counselor at the community college.

Practice 3

1. c   2. e   3. a   4. b   5. d

Practice 4

1. Jim wants a job which has health insurance.

2. All fish need water that is not polluted.

3. Sushi is a Japanese food that has raw (uncooked) fish in it.

4. I do not have a job that has a retirement plan.

Practice 5

1. who live in Layfayette, Indiana	circled: people
2. which was found in the water	circled: coliform bacteria
3. which had to be cleaned	circled: reservoir
4. that becomes polluted	circled: water
5. who have questions about their water	circled: people

Practice 7

1. who was the king's only daughter	circled: princess
2. who wins	circled: god
3. who became very angry	circled: loser
4. which is in July and August	circled: season

Practice 8

1. The god who won married the princess.

2. Summer is the season which has the most rain.

3. People say that the river god is jealous.

4. The god who lost became very angry.

Practice 9

1. c   2. c   3. a   4. b   5. a   6. b

REPRODUCIBLE MASTER
UNIT 7   # PROGRESS CHECK A

SPEAK OR WRITE

Look at the pictures from Unit 7. Use the questions below to talk or write about each picture.

Questions

1. What is this man's occupation?

2. Why isn't he successful?

3. What will happen to him?

LISTEN

While you listen, write a check under *True* or *False*.

	True	False
1. This story explains why there are kings in Vietnam.	_____	_____
2. This story is about two gods who fought for a princess.	_____	_____
3. The river god won the fight.	_____	_____
4. The mountain god protected the princess.	_____	_____
5. Today the river god has become friends with the mountain god.	_____	_____

REPRODUCIBLE MASTER
UNIT 7   PROGRESS CHECK B

LANGUAGE STRUCTURES

Combine the sentences. Use relative clauses with *who*, *which*, and *that*.

1. I have a new neighbor. She is from St. Louis, Missouri.

   _____

2. Our houses are next door to each other. They are on a lake.

   _____

3. Betty has three sons. All of them are married.

   _____

4. Her oldest son owns a computer software business. The business is very successful.

   _____

5. Her youngest son lives in Maine. He is a lobster fisherman.

   _____

CONTENT

Circle the letter of the correct answer.

1. Water pollution in the United States is
   a. a serious problem   b. a minor problem   c. not a problem.

2. Which of the following is not an endangered fish?
   a. swordfish   b. bluefin tuna   c. salmon

3. Why shouldn't restaurants serve swordfish?
   a. It doesn't taste good.
   b. It's disappearing from the oceans.
   c. It's too expensive.

4. Which is not a dessert?
   a. chocolate cake   b. cheesecake   c. crab cake

5. Where can you find a job counselor?
   a. at a community college   b. at a bank   c. at a newspaper

Name _____ Date _____

ACTIVITY MASTER 7-1

MORE READING FOR REAL

Six Great Lakes?

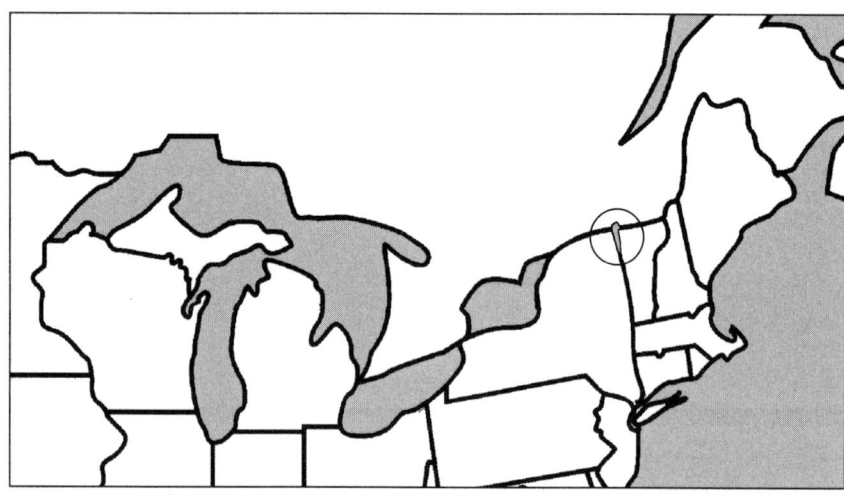

Read the questions below. Then read the map and the story. Answer the questions.

Six Great Lakes?

What makes a lake great? A bill that President Clinton signed on March 6, 1998, added Lake Champlain to the Great Lakes. Vermont Senator, Patrick Leahy, was responsible for the bill that Clinton signed. Lawmakers who were from the five Great Lakes states were so angry that the bill was changed two weeks later.

Lake Champlain is named for Samuel Champlain, the French explorer who founded Quebec, Canada. What makes Lake Champlain great? It's not size. Lake Champlain is about one-sixteenth the size of Lake Ontario, the smallest of the five Great Lakes.

People who live in Vermont, where Lake Champlain is located, have several reasons for calling Lake Champlain "great." It is part of the same drainage basin as the other Great Lakes. It was formed by the same glaciers. And it has the same problems.

So, how many Great Lakes are there? It depends where you live. Midwesterners will continue to count five lakes, but New Englanders will probably count six!

Now mark *True* or *False* next to each sentence. Circle the correct information in the map and story. Correct the false sentences in your notebook. Write two more sentences to ask another pair.

	True	False
1. Lake Champlain is named for a French explorer.	_____	_____
2. Lake Champlain is one of the five Great Lakes.	_____	_____
3. Lake Champlain is on the border of Vermont and Pennsylvania.	_____	_____
4. Patrick Leahy is the President of the United States.	_____	_____
5. Lake Champlain is larger than Lake Ontario.	_____	_____

Name _____ Date _____

SENTENCE BUILDING WITH RELATIVE CLAUSES

Directions: Work with a partner or group. Match the beginnings of sentences with the ends of sentences. Write two sentence beginnings on the blank cards. Ask your teacher to check your sentences. Give the unfinished sentences to another pair or group. Ask that group to complete the sentences using relative clauses.

✂

I have a friend	who works three jobs.
We found a house	that we want to buy.
She has a job	that she hates.
He has a boss	that he likes a lot.
I bought a book	that was on the best seller list.
We moved to neighborhood	which has many parks.
That's my uncle	who is a pilot.
Our city has a mayor	who is concerned about water pollution.
Do you know	which VCR you want to buy?
I use a computer	which is easy to operate.

Unit 8 Saving Money for the Future

OVERVIEW

Objectives

Skills and Structures

Talk about people's problems

Understand bank advertisements

Read tips for starting a business

Talk about benefits

Read a bar graph and a line graph

Read and solve problems

Use a T-chart to present ideas

Use direct and indirect objects

Use embedded questions

SCANS Competencies

Acquire and evaluate information: Student Book, Sound Bites, page 86, Sound Bites, page 91; Workbook, page 47; Identify and allocate resources (Money): Student Book, Culture Corner, page 90; Student Book, Wrap Up, page 96; Workbook, page 48; Interpret and communicate information: Teacher's Manual, p.127 (Notes on Reading for Real)

Realia

Employee handbooks

Employment ads describing benefits such as life insurance and 401(k)s

Bank and credit union brochures describing services and interest rates

ATM card

ACTIVITY NOTES

Page 85

Scene 1

Preparation

1. Ask students "Who has a bank account? Who does not?" List and discuss reasons why people have or do not have accounts.

2. On the board make an idea map with *How to Save Money for the Future* in the center. With the class, brainstorm ideas. The resulting idea map could be made into a class poster which could be added to over the course of the unit.

Extension

Have pairs of students role-play the Scene in one of several ways. Bring in props or costumes to make the activity more interesting, If possible, videotape the role plays and have students critique their own performances.

Option 1: Students can perform the lines as written. You can assign pairs or let students choose their own partners.

Option 2: Students can make a simple substitution in some lines (by inserting the name of a nearby apartment complex or subdivision, for example).

Option 3: More advanced students can ad-lib a conversation on the topic treated in the Scene, or pretend that they are one of Thi's neighbors and are also being interviewed.

Page 86

Sound Bites

Before You Listen

Preparation

1. On the board write some of the key terms from the listening exercise: *interest, loan, investment,* and *retirement.* Read each description or definition below and have students call out the vocabulary item it describes.
   - amounts of money paid in order to make more money later (investment)
   - stopping work at age 55–65 (retirement)
   - money you borrow and pay back later (loan)
   - the percentage of money you get back from money put into the bank (interest)

2. Ask learners, "Have you ever borrowed money from a bank? What kinds of loans do banks give?" Elicit learners' background knowledge and experience before looking at the brochure.

While You Listen

Presentation

Before playing the tape, have students look over the pictures. Answer any questions they have.

After You Listen

Extension

Divide into groups and distribute a brochure from a different bank or credit union to each group. Have each group study the brochure and make a "sales pitch" to the class about each institution. Then vote with the class on which institution offers the best services. Tally votes on the board.

Answers to Sound Bites

2	5
1	3
4	6

Listening Script

1. The Veches always loved to make pizza, and now they've finally decided to open their own pizzeria. So why have they stopped worrying and started enjoying themselves? They applied for a small business loan at AmFederal, with a modest interest rate and manageable monthly payments. At AmFederal, we'll lend you a helping hand.

2. Is the roof on your new dream home not quite what you expected? Is the price of new windows giving you high blood pressure? How about that deck you've always wanted to build? UrbanBank has a full line of home equity loans to help you make that dream home a reality. Don't let the roof cave in on your dreams. Contact UrbanBank today.

3. Your third child was just born. College seems a long way off, but at approximately $24,000 a year for four years times three, you've got to start thinking about it now. At Taylor Finance, we'll show you ways to increase your money, such as putting 70% into large-cap stocks and 30% into bonds. Prepare for those big college bills. Call Taylor Finance today, and look forward to tomorrow.

4. Some people are still on the go after age 65. In fact, it's just the beginning for them. They've got places to go, adventures ahead, and a retirement plan to finance the exciting years to come. At Richmond Retirement Services, we've got the package you need, whether it's IRAs, 401(k)s, annuities, or life insurance. We promise you a future where the best is yet to come. Call Richmond for a free brochure.

5. Are you kidding? They charge you a monthly fee for your checking account? And you don't earn any interest? Look, I just opened an account with Hometown . . . yeah, Hometown Savings . . and I've got free checking, market-rate interest, and ATM access all over town! . . What? . . . Sure, I'll give you the number . .

6. Wife: Honey! That house across the street is for sale!

   Husband: Yeah, but. . .

   Wife: My mother's thinking of moving, and it looks just the right size for all of us!

   Husband: But . . .

   Wife: You know, Harrison Mutual is offering first-time homeowners' loans with super-low interest rates!

   Husband: Well, I . . .

   Wife: There's just a 5% downpayment, so let's call Harrison Mutual today and get an application—we can surprise my mother!

   Husband: Can I ask you a question?

   Wife: . . . Sure.

   Husband: Where's the aspirin?

Page 87

Spotlight on Direct and Indirect Objects

Preparation

1. Introduce direct and indirect objects by writing the following unfinished sentence on the board: "I sent a letter _____." Ask students to label the subject (*I*) and the verb (*sent*) of the sentence. Explain that in this sentence, *a letter* is the direct object because it is the thing being sent. It is directly affected by the verb. Label the parts of speech with S, V, and DO.

   Next, ask students to try to finish the sentence. Here is an example: "I sent a letter to my mother." Explain that *my mother* is the indirect object because she is receiving the letter—she is only indirectly affected by the verb because she is not the thing being sent. Label *my mother* with the letters IO.

2. Write some other simple sentences and have students label the parts of speech. Use verbs such as *give, send,* and *lend.*

3. To introduce the optional word order, ask students to move *my mother* to another part of the sentence—for example, write, "I sent my mother a letter." Again, ask students to label the parts of speech to see that the direct and indirect objects remain the same—only the word order has changed. Note also that the preposition *to* is dropped. With the sentences the students have previously generated, have students try to change the word order.

Presentation

After students have read the examples in the Spotlight Box, have them complete sentences such as the following and then label the parts of speech:

- I asked my boss _____.
- I gave my friend _____.
- I saved _____ some money.
- I owe _____ $5.00.

Answers to Exercise 1

1. <u>a bonus</u> (my whole department)
   The owner of the company gave my whole department a bonus.

2. <u>some money</u> (my family)
   I need to send my family some money.

3. <u>$5.00</u> (my friend John)
   I lent my friend John $5.00 the other day.

4. <u>money</u> (your family)
   You can save your family money with these coupons.

Answers to Exercise 2

1. This noise is giving me a headache.

2. Ask your boss questions when you don't understand.

3. They offered me a job after the interview.

4. The bank charges me when I make late payments.

Workbook

Workbook pages 43 and 44 may be assigned after students have completed Student Book page 87.

Person to Person

Preparation

In small groups, have students quickly scan the conversations for unfamiliar words and share them with the class. If no one can provide a definition or example, explain the word. Students' unfamiliar words may include the following: *bounced, overdraft fee, application fee,* and *pretty good.*

Reading for Real

Preparation

In small groups have students come up with their own description or definition of *small business.* Have a volunteer from each group share the definition with the class. Write students' ideas on the board, clarifying them if necessary. Make a class definition. Leave it on the board for students to refer to throughout the reading.

Presentation

Depending on the level of your students, you may want to present and discuss the reading point by point.

Extension

1. Assign each point in the article to a different group. Have groups prepare an explanation and give examples of each point to the rest of the class.

2. If possible, have a small-business owner visit the class for a question/answer session. Ask student groups to prepare a list of questions before the visit.

Answers to Exercise 3

1. T   2. F   3. F   4. F   5. F

Page 90

Culture Corner

Preparation

In pairs have students do a word association with the word *benefits*. For one minute, one student will call out all the words he or she associates with *benefits* while the partner writes them down. Tell students there is no right or wrong answer, so they should not try to edit themselves. Then have students switch roles. Tell students to combine their list with their partner's. Ask volunteers to read the combined lists to the class.

Presentation

After students have talked about the meanings of the terms in the chart, read down the list of benefits together and elicit a definition or explanation from students. Check by asking questions such as the following:

- Which one means money you are paid if you get sick or hurt? (disability insurance)

- Which one means that your company pays your expenses for going to school? (educational reimbursement)

- Which one means that if the company makes a lot of money, you will receive some extra pay? (profit sharing or stock purchase plan)

Exercise 4

Presentation

If students are not currently employed, have them use information from a spouse or parent's job.

Extension

Extend the activity by bringing in copies of an employee handbook and/or want ads (discuss abbreviations if needed). Look at the benefits being offered. Have students compare them with their own benefits.

Scene 2

Preparation

1. Quickly review the story line from Scene 1. Say, "There was a fire in an apartment complex, and Thi Hyung lost all the money her family had lent her to start a business. She was very depressed and upset."

2. With the class discuss what Thi should do now. Ask students what they would do if they suddenly lost a large sum of money.

Extension

Have pairs of students role-play the Scene in one of several ways. Bring in props or costumes to make the activity more interesting, If possible, videotape the role plays and have students critique their own performances.

 Option 1: Students can perform the lines as written. You can assign pairs or let students choose their own partners.

Option 2: Students can make a simple substitution in some lines (by inserting another benefit of banking, for example).

Option 3: More advanced students can ad-lib a conversation on the topic treated in the Scene, or pretend that they are in the conversation with Thi and Rhoun.

Sound Bites

While You Listen

Preparation

Ask students, "Have you ever opened a bank account? Was it easy or difficult? What different kinds of accounts do banks offer?" Share the learners' experience and knowledge.

After You Listen

Extension

1. After students have discussed the answers, play the tape again so that they can clarify any areas they did not understand.

2. If possible, invite a bank or credit union representative to explain the services they offer and to answer questions. As an alternative, take a trip to the institution and also visit an ATM (automatic teller machine) at the bank and elsewhere to see how it functions.

Answers to Sound Bites

Answers may vary. Here are some possible answers:

Thi wants to open a checking and a savings account.

Direct deposit is a method whereby a person's employer sends an employee's paycheck directly to the bank account. It is offered by some banks and some employers.

An ATM card will allow Thi to get money from either of her accounts at any of her bank's machines. Thi will talk to Bill in the bank's loan department.

Listening Script

Nadine:	Hello, my name is Nadine. How may I help you?
Thi:	(*Sounds hesitant throughout*) I think I'd like to open an account.
Nadine:	What kind of an account?
Thi:	I don't know what kind of account I want. Can you explain the different kinds to me?
Nadine:	Well, we have a variety of accounts—savings, checking, money market, etc.
Thi:	Oh, I want to open a checking account and a savings account. How much does it cost?
Nadine:	We have many different kinds of checking accounts. Some have service charges and some don't.
Thi:	I don't understand. How do I know which one is best for me?
Nadine:	Let me explain a few options to you. If you keep a minimum balance of $250 in your checking account, there is no monthly fee. Or if your paycheck is direct-deposited, there is no monthly fee.
Thi:	I'm not sure what direct-deposited means.
Nadine:	That's when your employer sends your paycheck directly to the bank. Does your employer offer that option?
Thi:	I don't know if the company does that or not.
Nadine:	Well, you can let us know later. You can also have an ATM card for both accounts. That way you can get money from your accounts at any of our bank machines.
Thi:	I see. I was also wondering whether you give loans to start a business?
Nadine:	Yes, we do. You can talk to Bill in our loan department.

Page 92

Spotlight on Embedded Questions

Preparation

1. With books closed, write the *wh*-question featured in the Spotlight Box on page 92: "Who can help me?" Ask students to label the subject (*Who*) and the verb (*can*) and ask them to finish this sentence: "I'm not sure . . . (who can help me)." Explain that the second half is now *embedded* in the sentence and the subject + verb order doesn't change in this case. Remind students that subject-object order does not change in embedded questions with *who*. Think of more questions that begin with *who* and change them to *I'm not sure . . .* embedded questions.

2. Write the question "How can I open a business?" Ask students to label the subject (*I*) and the verb (*can*), which are in verb + subject order. Then ask students to finish the following sentence: "Please tell me . . . (how I can open a business)." Point out how the word order changes from verb + subject to subject + verb. Think of more questions with *how, what,* and *where,* and change them into *Please tell me . . .* embedded questions.

Presentation

Review the sentences in the Spotlight Box with the class. Emphasize when the word order changes.

Extension

Divide the class into Group A and Group B. Have someone from Group A ask a *Who, What* or *Where . . .?* question and someone from Group B makes it more polite by using a sentence starter such as the following: "Could you tell me . . .?" or "Do you know . . . ?" If the embedded question is correct, Group B gets a point. Now Group B asks a *wh*-question and Group A must form the embedded question. The team with the most points wins.

Answers to Exercise 5

                   S V
1. Can you tell me how I can open an account?

                       S   V
2. I'm not sure which bank I should go to.

                     S   V
3. Do you know what happened to my application?

                     S   V
4. I need to know where I can get an application.

                     S   V
5. Please tell me what my balance is.

Your Turn

Extension

Tell students they are going to use their questions to choose a bank. You will answer three questions from each group. Based on your answers, they must decide whether or not to use your bank.

Workbook

Workbook page 45 may be assigned after students have completed Student Book page 92.

Page 93

Spotlight on More Embedded Questions: Yes/No Questions and Infinitives

Preparation

1. With books closed, write the *wh*-question featured in the Spotlight Box on page 93, "Do I have enough money?" Point out that this is a Yes/No question. Ask students to finish the following sentence: "I wonder . . . (if/whether I have enough money)." Explain that Yes/No questions will use *if* or *whether* in the embedded question and that the helping verb *Do* disappears. Think of more questions with *Do . . .?* and *Did . . .?* and change them to *I wonder . . .* with embedded questions.

2. To introduce the use of the infinitive, write on the board, "Should I go?" Ask students to finish the following sentence: "I'm not sure . . .(if/whether I should go)."

Now say that you want to make the sentence shorter. What word do you need in the blank? "I'm not sure whether _____ (to) go." Point out that questions with the meanings *can* and *should* can be shortened by using the infinitive in this way. Think of more questions with *Where can I . . .?, How should I . . .?* and change them into *I'm not sure . . .* with embedded questions.

Presentation

With the class review the examples in the Spotlight Box. Emphasize the word order and the implied meaning of using the infinitive.

Answers to Exercise 7

1. Do you know who I should write the check to? Do you know who to write the check to?

2. I'm not sure if I should invest money in the stock market. I'm not sure whether to invest money in the stock market.

3. I'd like to know where I can get more information. I'd like to know where to get more information.

Workbook

Workbook page 46 may be assigned after students have completed page 93.

Page 94

Get Graphic

Preparation

With the class talk about saving money. Is it more important in the students' native countries or in the United States? Do students think it is easier or more difficult to save money in the United States? Why?

Presentation

Read the direction paragraph with the class. Be sure students understand what the two graphs represent before they concentrate on the numbers.

Answers to Exercise 8

1. 9%	2. 4%	3. up	4. 1981	5. 1982	6. 1984
7. 5%	8. lower	9. 13%	10. 8%		

Activity Masters

Activity Master 8-1 may be introduced after students have completed Student Book page 94.

Preparation

1. Explain the terms *risk* (possibility of losing some money on your investment) and *potential rate of return* (possible profit you can make by investing money). The *risk* and the *potential rate of return* may be higher or lower with each kind of investment fund. Before investing in anything, students should ask themselves the following question: "Is the risk worth the possible profit?"

2. Survey the class. Have students raise their hands if they currently have some kind of investment. Use these students as group leaders.

Issues and Answers

Preparation

Tell students they have been offered a new job. Have them write one benefits question that they think is the most important. Ask volunteers to write their questions on the board. Leave them there for the extension activity.

Extension

In groups, have students develop real questions to ask either at the Human Resources Office of their workplace or at their bank. Together, write the questions on an overhead transparency and correct any errors. When students respond with the answers to these questions, have a sharing session.

Wrap-Up

Presentation

With the class, talk about how people can reduce or control either their fixed or flexible expenses. What is absolutely necessary to spend each month and what isn't? On the board make a T-chart with ideas.

Workbook

Workbook pages 47 and 48 may be assigned after students have completed Student Book page 96.

Activity Masters

Activity Master 8-2 may be introduced after students have completed Student Book page 96. This is a review activity which pulls together embedded questions and much of the content in the chapter.

Presentation

Directions: Cut out the squares and distribute randomly in the class. Students must pair up and ask their questions with polite sentence starters such as *Do you know . . .?* or *Could you tell me . . .?* with correct embedded questions. The other student answers the question. The two students exchange cards and continue to pair up with different partners. After 10 minutes, each student must find a partner and read their question and answer aloud to the class. There is one card marked your question for which students must supply their own question.

ANSWERS TO PROGRESS CHECKS

Progress Check A

Speak or Write

Answers will vary. Here are some possible answers:

1. Thi has lost all her money in the big fire.

2. She was going to start a business, but now she can't.

3. She could have put her money in the bank instead of under her mattress.

Listening Script

Three quarters of Americans are in debt. Only one out of four people does not owe money. Most families have four-figure mortgage payments to make each month. That's more than a thousand dollars.

Most American families *do* have some money to spend, however. The average family income is more than $44,000. Of that, Americans spend about $32,000. That leaves some extra cash.

In fact, two-thirds of Americans have extra money to spend.

Listen

1. Three quarters
2. one out of four
3. more than a thousand
4. $44,000
5. $32,000
6. two-thirds

Progress Check B

Language Structures

A. Direct objects (underlined): a sweater, a pair of jeans, shoes, bars of soap, very little money

Indirect objects (circled): his mother, his brother, his nieces and nephews, all his aunts and uncles

B. 1. how to save money
   2. who can help me
   3. whether to go to a bank
   4. what questions to ask

Content

1. j   2. g   3. i   4. e   5. f   6 a   7. d   8. h   9. b   10. c

ANSWERS TO ACTIVITY MASTERS

Activity Master 8-1

1. False   2. True   3. False   4. True   5. True

Activity Master 8-2

(*Do you know/Could you tell me . . .*)

. . . what interest is?

. . . what home equity loans are for?

. . . when you're going to retire?

. . . what disability insurance is?

. . . what educational reimbursement is?

. . . what direct deposit is?

. . . what the difference is between a checking and a savings account?

. . . how life insurance works?

. . . why it's important to have health insurance?

. . . what 401(K)s are?

. . . how ATM cards work?

. . . what fixed expenses are?

. . . what flexible expenses are?

. . . what Americans spend most of their money on?

. . . what charities are?

Name _____ Date _____

WORKBOOK ANSWERS

Practice 1
1. <u>a postcard</u> (you) 2. <u>money</u> 3. <u>money</u> 4. <u>interest</u> (me) 5. <u>money</u> 6. <u>money</u>

Practice 2
Answers will vary. Here are some possible answers:

1. She loaned her brother $250.

2. She sent her mother $100.

3. She gave her church $10.

4. She bought her daughter a new car.

Practice 3
1. for   2. for   3. to   4. for   5. to

Practice 5
1. who her supervisor is

2. what she is supposed to do

3. where she can find supplies

4. when she has break

5. what she should be doing now

Practice 6
1. what the injury was

2. what happened

3. who was there at the time

4. when the accident took place

5. what help the employee got

Practice 7
1. how to fill out W-2 forms

2. when they can expect their first checks

3. whether to set up direct deposit

4. how to apply for benefits

5. whether to buy safety shoes

Practice 8
1. what the cross streets are?

2. what routes to take?

3. where to park?

Practice 9
1. True   2. False   3. False   4. True   5. False

Name _____ Date _____

SPEAK OR WRITE

Look at the pictures from Unit 8. Use the questions below to talk or
write about each picture. Retell the story in your own words.

Questions

1. Why is Thi so upset?

2. What had she planned to do?

3. What could Thi have done to avoid this tragedy?

LISTEN

While you listen, write the correct number or fraction.

_____ of Americans are in debt. Only _____ people does not

owe money. Most families have four-figure mortgage payments.

That's _____ dollars. Most American families do have some money

to spend, however. The average family income is more than _____.

Of that, Americans spend about _____. That leaves some extra

cash. In fact, _____ of Americans have extra money to spend.

UNIT 8   PROGRESS CHECK B

LANGUAGE STRUCTURES

A. Underline the *direct objects* and circle the *indirect objects* in the story below.

Fung traveled to his country last year. He didn't want to go there empty-handed. He gave his mother a sweater. He gave his brother a pair of jeans. He bought shoes for his nieces and nephews. He decided to give bars of soap to all his aunts and uncles since he had very little money left to spend!

B. Change the questions below into embedded questions. Use infinitives wherever possible.

1. How can I save money?
   I want to know _____.

2. Who can help me?
   I wonder _____.

3. Should I go to a bank?
   I'm not sure _____.

4. What questions should I ask?
   I don't know _____.

CONTENT

Match the word or words with the correct explanation. Put the correct letter in the blank.

1. Interest _____   a. is a matching investment plan.

2. A home equity loan _____   b. is a machine for getting cash.

3. Retirement _____   c. is your salary when you retire.

4. Life insurance _____   d. means your company helps you pay for school.

5. Disability insurance _____ e. can help your family if you die.

6. A 401 (K) _____   f. can help if you're sick or hurt.

7. Educational
   reimbursement _____   g. is to improve your house.

8. Direct deposit _____   h. means your company sends your paycheck to your bank.

9. An ATM _____   i. is the time when you stop working.

10. A pension _____   j. is extra money you earn.

Name _____ Date _____

MORE GRAPHIC SKILLS

Investing: Potential Risk Vs. Return

Rhoun works in a factory that offers retirement investing. Each month, employees put part of their paycheck into investment funds of their choice. Look at the bar graph and help Rhoun decide which fund to invest in.

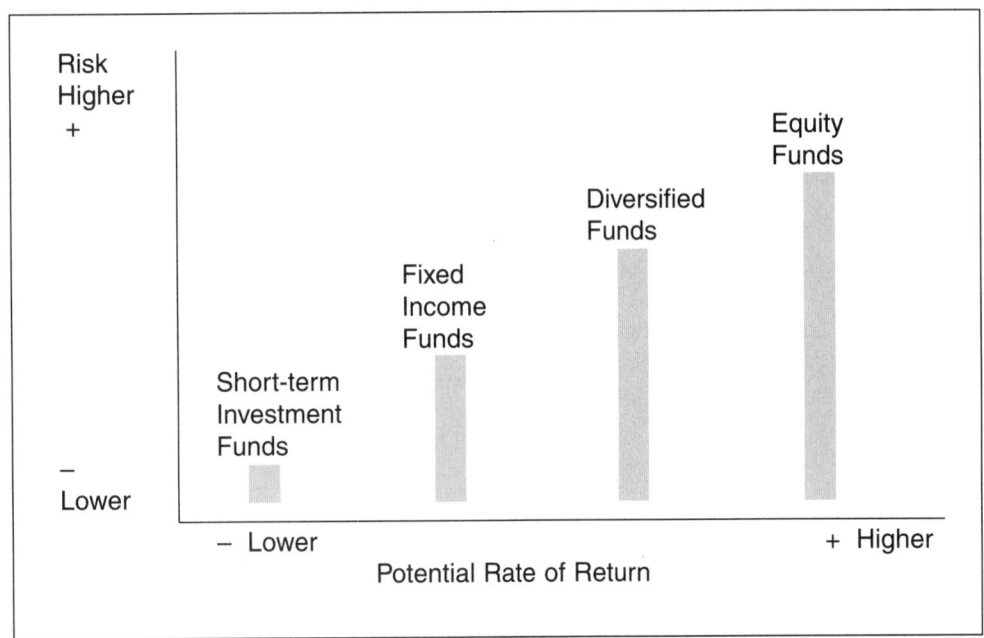

Answer the questions. Put a check under *True* or *False*.

	True	False
1. Short-term investment funds are the safest place to put your money, and you can earn the most.	_____	_____
2. Equity Funds are the riskiest place to put your money.	_____	_____
3. You can make more money in Diversified Funds than in Fixed Income Funds, and they are safer.	_____	_____
4. People who have extra money and who don't care about risk should choose Equity Funds.	_____	_____
5. Rhoun is very nervous about investing her money, and she would be happy making only a small profit. She should choose Short-term investment funds.	_____	_____

REPRODUCIBLE MASTER
UNIT 8
ACTIVITY MASTER 8-2

SENTENCE BUILDING WITH EMBEDDED QUESTIONS

Note: For complete directions for this activity, see Teacher's Manual page 133.

✂

What is interest?

What are home equity loans for?

When are you going to retire?

What is disability insurance?

What is educational reimbursement?

What is direct deposit?

What's the difference between a checking and a savings account?

How does life insurance work?

Why is it important to have health insurance?

What are 401(K)s?

How does an ATM card work?

What are fixed expenses?

What are flexible expenses?

What do Americans spend most of their money on?

What are charities?

(your question)

GETTING HELP IN YOUR COMMUNITY

OVERVIEW

Objectives

Skills and Structures

Talk about people's problems

Understand conversations about problems

Understand community resources

Read a college brochure

Understand parenting advice

Read pie charts

Read and write about sexual harassment

Use an idea map

Use time clauses

Use clauses of cause/effect

Use clauses of opposition

SCANS Competencies

Acquire and evaluate information: Student Book, Sound Bites, page 98; Student Book, Sound Bites, page 103; Student Book, Reading for Real, page 101; Workbook, page 53; Problem-Solving: Student Book, Culture Corner, page 102; Student Book, Get Graphic, page 106; Student Book, Issues and Answers, page 107; Student Book, Wrap Up, page 108; Workbook, page 54

Reasoning (Cause/Effect and Opposition): Student Book, Spotlight on Clauses of Cause/Effect, page 104, Spotlight on Clauses of Opposition, page 105; Workbook, pages 49 and 50

Realia

Brochures or flyers from local community resource centers or immigrant advocacy organizations

Catalogs or schedules for college classes or vocational training

Recent articles about sexual harassment

ACTIVITY NOTES

Page 97

Scene 1

Preparation

Make a T-chart with two headings, *Raising children in my country* and *Raising children in the United States.* With the class, brainstorm what students perceive as the differences in child-rearing and family attitudes in general. Ask, "Are parents more strict or less strict in your country? What happens when there are serious problems in the family?" Focus on how problems get solved. A possible extension to the discussion might be questions such as the following: "What problems might parents have with their children as they move from their native country to the United States?"

Extension

Have individual students talk about the Scene from different points of view. Bring in props or costumes to make the activity more interesting.

Option 1: Students can tell what happened from Miguel's point of view.

Option 2: Students can tell what happened from Celia's point of view

Option 3: More advanced students can ad-lib a conversation about the incident between two neighbors.

Sound Bites

While You Listen

Preparation

In small groups have students list the local community resources they are familiar with, if any.

Presentation

1. Read over the directions with the class. Answer any questions.
2. Remind students that they only need to write a number.

After You Listen

Extension

Distribute brochures or flyers from local community resource centers or immigrant advocacy organizations. Familiarize students with the kinds of services each provides.

Option 1: Describe some problems and have students call out the service needed. For example, say, " I speak only Korean, and I have to go to court." (Translators/ Interpreters)

Option 2: Have one group of students write problems on a strip of paper and have another group search for a community resource to address that problem.

Listening Script

1. My name is Celia. I have a two-year-old son, Miguel, and I also have an 8-month-old boy. The other day, Miguel let the baby outside, and he fell down the stairs. All the neighbors were watching. I got really mad at Miguel, but I know he's only two. When he's bad like that, I lose my temper and it makes things worse. I'm really going crazy.

2. My name is Connie and . . . I really need some help. Everything was OK until my husband lost his job a few months ago. He gets angry pretty easily; but once he got fired, he got worse. When he came home, he started fighting with me for no reason, and we both started shouting. But lately he's been pushing me too. I'm afraid to be in my own home.

3. I'm Michael. I know I have a problem. I have a boring job, but I can't get out of it. Anyway, I used to drink after I came home from work. Or I had a beer with other people . . . but then I started drinking alone. And now I drink before I go to work, too. I know I'm going to lose my job—soon—if I don't do something about my drinking problem.

4. My name is Ursula. I don't know what's been wrong with me since my aunt died. As long as I can remember, she was like a mother to me. I keep thinking about her. I can't eat, I can't sleep—even though I'm always tired—and I can't concentrate on anything. I don't know what to do.

5. I'm Andrea. As soon as I found out I was pregnant, I panicked. We just got married three months ago, and we planned to save a lot more money before we started a family. Now we'll probably have to borrow money from our parents. In any case, I haven't even seen a doctor yet. I don't know where to find one.

6. My name is Kishor. My wife and I called to schedule an appointment to see a condominium. The manager seemed very friendly while we were talking on the phone. Things changed once we got to the office, however. The man looked at us, and I knew he didn't want us to see the condo. He made excuses about the building being under repair. Why didn't he mention that before? I talked to my brother, who is a lawyer, and he said to call you.

7. My name is Alex Price. I think there's something strange going on in the apartment next door. Whenever I come home, I hear a lot of yelling, and the other day the kid . . . he's ten, I think . . . he came out with a black eye. I don't know, maybe it's none of my business. Anyway, I'm calling because it really bothered me.

8. My name is Mark. I'm worried about my son. He used to do well in school, but now his grades are bad. As soon as he gets home every day, he goes to his room and locks the door. I think he needs to meet other kids, but he won't listen to me.

Answers to Sound Bites

1. 326   2. 321   3. 328   4. 323   5. 327   6. 324

7. 322   8. 330 or 326

Page 99

Spotlight on Time Clauses

Preparation

Introduce time clauses by asking students to combine the following sentences:

- I called the airline.
- I went to the airport.

If necessary, hint that the word *before* is needed. Point out that the resulting sentence can be written in either of the following two ways:

- I called the airline before I went to the airport.
- Before I went to the airport, I called the airline.

Explain that the *before* . . . part of the sentence (whether it comes at the beginning or the end) is called a *time clause.* It answers the question *when?* Write another example sentence pair on the board, one sentence with the time clause at the beginning, and one sentence with the time clause at the end. Elicit from the students the rule that a comma is needed when the time clause comes at the beginning of the sentence.

Presentation

After reading the examples in the Spotlight Box, check the learners' understanding by reproducing the six model sentences on a separate of paper—but *omitting* the adverb clause in each sentence. Have learners complete each sentence with the correct adverb clause. This activity should help learners distinguish between *before, while,* and *after* sequences as well as acquaint them with the variety of verb patterns that can accompany time clauses.

Extension

Have students think of a major event that happened in their life, such as getting married, having children, or coming to the United States. Have them think about how things were *before, when,* and *after* the event occurred. Then, together, write sentences with time clauses. For homework, ask students to use those sentences to write a paragraph about a major life event.

Answers to Exercise 1

Answers will vary. Here are some possible answers:

1. Since
2. By the time
3. Whenever
4. as soon as
5. Before
6. After
7. until

Workbook

Workbook page 49 may be assigned after students have completed Student Book page 99.

Page 100

Person to Person

Extension

Have students role-play the dialogues in several ways. Bring in props or costumes to make the activity more interesting.

 Option 1: Students can perform a dialogue as written. They can choose their own dialogue, or you can assign them.

Option 2: Students can write additional lines for the characters and present the combined dialogue to the class.

Page 101

Reading for Real

Preparation

In small groups have students discuss what kind of information would be found in a college brochure or catalog. Discuss this with the class.

Extension

Research options for taking college courses or vocational training in the community. Have groups of students select a particular school. Have them study catalogs or call the institution to find out the following information:

- What are the entrance requirements?
- How much does it cost?
- What is the enrollment deadline for the next class?

Have groups report back to the class. If possible, tour a college or training center, or schedule a visit by an academic counselor. Ask the counselor to discuss long- and short-term goals. What are the steps students need to take now to reach their long-term goals?

Exercise 2

Extension

Have students correct the false sentences in their notebooks.

Answers to Exercise 2

1. True   2. False   3. True   4. True   5. False

Page 102

Culture Corner

Preparation

Ask students, "What should parents do when their children misbehave (fight, do bad things, do not listen)? Are child-rearing and disciplining different in your country? In what way?" Discuss this with the class before reading the article.

Presentation

After students read the selection, discuss any vocabulary students did not understand before discussing content.

Extension

In groups, discuss gender differences in parenting, both in the United States and in students' native countries. Do mothers play a different role from fathers in making children obey and teaching right and wrong? Have individual students write a short paragraph on the subject. Then duplicate several interesting paragraphs on a single page and distribute for a general class discussion. Writers should be anonymous.

Page 103

Scene 2

Preparation

1. In small groups have students read the sentence above the comic strip. Ask, "If you are having trouble with children, where do you go for help?"

2. Quickly review the story line from Scene 1. Celia was in the shower, and her two-year-old son, Miguel, opened the door and let the baby crawl outside. The baby fell down the stairs, and Celia yelled at Miguel in front of the neighbors. She is upset, angry, and embarrassed.

Extension

Have individual students role-play the Scene in one of several ways. Bring in props or costumes to make the activity more interesting, If possible, videotape the role plays so that students can critique their own performances.

 Option 1: Students can perform the lines as written. Students can choose their own partners, or you can assign them.

Option 2: Students can make a simple substitution in some lines (by inserting another problem, for example)

Option 3: More advanced students can pretend they are members of the parents' support group, and give Celia more advice.

Sound Bites

While You Listen

Preparation

Tell learners, "This is a conversation that takes place a few months later between Celia and a friend of hers from the support group. What do you think they will say? Do you think anything has changed?" Elicit some ideas and hypotheses before listening.

After You Listen

Extension

In groups, have students discuss the following questions:

- How did my parents affect me?
- Am I the same as or different from them now? In what ways?

If students do not want to talk about their own childhood, make the questions more general. Here is an example. " How can parents affect children?" Have groups generate some ideas and share them with the class through an idea map on the board.

Listening Script

Celia: Lupe? Hi. . . This is Celia.

Lupe: *Celia!* How are you doing?

Celia: OK. Can you talk?

Lupe: Sure! I haven't heard from you in a long time. We miss you in the group.

Celia: Yeah, I got a new job. I'm so busy.

Lupe: So how are things going?

Celia: Pretty good, actually. Something kind of neat happened the other day.

Lupe: Yeah?

Celia: Yeah, Miguel . . . you know he's almost four now . . . he was outside, and he started fighting with his younger brother over some toy . . .

Lupe: Uh huh?

Celia: . . . and I ran out there. I didn't yell even though I felt like it. Instead, I asked them why they were fighting. Then I showed them a game to play together with the toy. By the time they started playing the game, they had forgotten all about fighting. My neighbor was there . . .

Lupe: And?

Celia: She said what a good mother I was. It felt so good to hear that.

Lupe: Celia, that's *wonderful.*

Celia: It's still hard sometimes, but—I think our family's going to be all right.

Answers to Sound Bites

Answers may vary. Here are some possible answers:

Celia's sons started to fight one day, but she was able to stop the fight. A neighbor saw what happened and said Celia was a good mother. Now she feels pretty good.

Page 104

Spotlight on Clauses of Cause and Effect

Preparation

With books closed write the following sentences on the board.

- I smoke.
- My parents smoked.

Ask students, "Which is the cause and which is the effect?" (number 2 = cause; number 1 = effect) Ask students to combine the sentences. If necessary, suggest the word *because*. As with the time clauses, explain that the sentence can be written in two ways. Have students note punctuation as you write the following sentences on the board:

- I smoke because my parents smoked.
- Because my parents smoked, I smoke.

Write several other cause and effect sentences with *because, since, as,* and *now that* (varying as to whether the clause comes first or second).

Ask students to label the cause and effect parts of each sentence.

Extension

Think of some cause and effect events (for example, "I enrolled in English classes; I wanted to get a better job.") and write them in simple sentences on separate strips of paper. Distribute them randomly in class. Have individuals circulate until they get into cause and effect pairs. Have them form sentences aloud with the clauses. The pairs can then move to the board and write their sentences.

Answers to Exercise 3

1. e   2. c   3. a   4. d   5. b

Workbook

Workbook page 50 may be assigned after students have completed Student Book page 104.

Spotlight on Clauses of Opposition

Preparation

1. Have students close their books. Write the following related sentences on the board:

   - I want to go to the movies every weekend.

   - It's too expensive.

   Ask students to tell you how the two sentences are related. (They are *opposing* ideas.) Now ask students to combine the sentences without using the word *but*. Resulting sentences might be something like the following:

   - I want to go to the movies every weekend although it's too expensive.

   - Although I want to go to the movies every weekend, it's too expensive.

2. Explain that unlike cause and effect words like *because,* opposition words like *although* can come in any order. There is usually a comma between the two parts, especially when the opposition clause comes first.

3. Think of some other opposing ideas and ask students to combine sentences using *although.*

Answers to Exercise 4

1. d   2. b   3. a   4. e   5. c

Workbook

Workbook pages 51 and 52 may be assigned after students have completed Student Book page 105.

Activity Masters

Activity Master 9-1 can be assigned after students have completed Student Book page 104.

Get Graphic

Preparation

With the class read the first two sentences in the directions. Ask students, Is this a problem in your country? Why or why not?"

Presentation

With the class read the directions. Review the pie charts and discuss any vocabulary the students are unsure of.

Extension

Discuss the incidence and effects of divorce in the United States versus in the students' native countries. Make a three-column chart with the headings *Reasons for Divorce, Problems Caused by Divorce,* and *Solutions.* With the class or in small groups, brainstorm ideas.

Answers to Exercise 5

1. True   2. False   3. False   4. True   5. True

Issues and Answers

Preparation

Ask learners, "What happens if someone talks to or touches a co-worker in a sexual way (that is unwanted)? What is this called? Is this illegal in your country? Share learners' knowledge and experiences before reading the newsletter.

Presentation

1. Depending on the level of your students, you may want to present the reading as a whole-class activity. Read and discuss each point before moving to the next.

2. Student questions and answers can be done in small groups.

Wrap-Up

Presentation

To help students generate specific ideas, redistribute the community resources brochures they used in the Extension activity for Sound Bites on Student Book page 98.

Workbook

Workbook pages 53 and 54 may be assigned after students have completed Student Book page 108.

Activity Masters

Activity Master 9-2 may also be introduced after students have completed Student Book page 108.

ANSWERS TO PROGRESS CHECKS

Progress Check A

Speak or Write

Answers will vary. Here are some possible answers:

1. Celia is at a parents' support group meeting.

2. She loses control of her anger. She can't help yelling. Her parents used to yell at her.

3. The leader tells her to ask for help so she can calm down before trying to help her kids.

Listening Script

Thank you for calling Hawthorne Community College. If you know your party's extension, you can dial anytime during this message. To reach Campus Police, press 1. For the Registrar's Office and billing information, press 2. For the library, press 3. For GED or ESL classes, press 4. For Disabled Student Services, press 5. For Concerts and Special Events, press 6. For the Computer Lab, press 7. For athletic events, hang up and dial (773) 555-3354. If you are calling from a rotary phone, please wait and an operator will assist you.

Listen

1. 3   2. 2   3. 5   4. 1   5. 4

Progress Check B

Language Structures

Answers will vary. Here are some possible answers:

1. I have no money because I lost my job.
2. When(ever) I think of my native country, I get homesick.
3. (Al)though I love motorcycles, I would never buy one myself.
4. While I was driving to work, I had a car accident.

Content

1. substance abuse   2. prenatal   3. battered   4. single parents
5. time-out   6. deadbeat   7. youth

ANSWERS FOR ACTIVITY MASTERS

Activity Master 9-1

Now that I have a home computer, I can use the Internet.

Although I usually cook a hot dinner for my family, sometimes I'm so tired from work that I order a pizza.

Two hundred people applied for the job, (al)though they knew their chances were not very good.

I like to relax and watch TV after I get home from work.

Carlos is a great person to work with, although he's very disorganized.

By the time I have my third child, I'll be 38 years old.

I left early for my appointment because I knew there would be a lot of traffic.

When I can speak and write English very well, _____ (answers will vary).

Activity Master 9-2

1. False   2. False   3. True   4. False   5. True

REPRODUCIBLE MASTER
Unit 9
WORKBOOK ANSWERS

Practice 1
1. c   2. d   3. b   4. e   5. a

Practice 3
Answers will vary. Here are some possible answers:

1. Some people have problems because they are poor.

2. Because they are fighting to survive, they don't have time for education.

3. They can't find good jobs because they don't have a good education.

4. Because they can't find good jobs, they feel frustrated.

5. They rob or steal because they have to pay for their needs.

Practice 5
Answers will vary. Here are some possible answers:

1. even though 2. Although/Though 3. whereas/although

4. while/whereas 5. Though/Although

Practice 6
Answers will vary. Here are some possible answers:

1. Although   4. because
2. Before   5. after/by the time
3. Although/Even though   6. while/when

Practice 7
1. Children's Learning Center   3. Waterville Medical Center
2. Comp-U-Save Inc.   4. Elm Grove Fitness Club

UNIT 9   PROGRESS CHECK A

SPEAK OR WRITE

Look at the pictures from Unit 9. Use the questions below to talk or write about each picture. Retell the story in your own words.

Questions

1. Where is Celia?

2. Why does Celia yell at her kids if she knows it's wrong?

3. Explain why the group leader gives the advice she does.

LISTEN

First read the statements/problems below. Then, while you listen to the recording from a community college, write the number of the correct extension to press.

                                                               Extension

1. I need to find a magazine article.   _____

2. I want to ask about my bill.   _____

3. I have a wheelchair. I need an elevator.   _____

4. I locked my keys in my car.   _____

5. I want to find out about English classes.   _____

PROGRESS CHECK B

LANGUAGE STRUCTURES

Combine the sentences below using an appropriate expression from the lists below. Be careful with punctuation.

Time	Cause/Effect	Opposition
before	because	while
after	since	though
when(ever)	now that	even though
while		although
by the time . . .		

1. I lost my job. I have no money.

   _____

2. I think of my home country. I get homesick.

   _____

3. I love motorcycles. I would never buy one myself.

   _____

4. I was driving to work. I had a car accident.

   _____

CONTENT

Look at the words below. Complete the sentences with the correct word(s). Be careful! There is one extra word.

battered   deadbeat   prenatal   single parents

sexual harassment   time-out   substance abuse   youth

There is help for troubled people at the Community Resource Center. People who take

drugs can call the (1) _____ hotline. Pregnant women can visit the

(2) _____ clinic. If there is hitting and violence at home, mothers and

children can stay at the (3) _____ women's shelter. The Center can help

(4) _____ who are trying to raise their children alone. The counselors explain

how to give children a (5) _____ when they are being very difficult. There is

also legal help for families with a (6) _____ parent who will not pay child

support. The (7) _____ center provides fun, interesting activities for

teenagers. There is help for all kinds of people.

REPRODUCIBLE MASTER
UNIT 9

ACTIVITY MASTER 9-1

SENTENCE BUILDING WITH CLAUSES

Directions: Work in pairs or groups of three. Cut out the sentences and phrases. Put them together to make logical sentences with clauses. Note that there is one unfinished sentence; write an ending on the blank strip of paper. Share answers with the class.

✂

Now that I have a home computer,
sometimes I'm so tired from work that I order a pizza.
Two hundred people applied for the job,
I like to relax and watch TV
although he's very disorganized.
I can use the Internet.
By the time I have my third child,
although they knew their chances were not very good.
I left early for my appointment
after I get home from work.
I'll be 38 years old.
Although I usually cook a hot dinner for my family,
When I can speak and write English very well,
because I knew there would be a lot of traffic.
Carlos is a great person to work with,

Name _____ Date _____

MORE READING FOR REAL

Crews—The New Gangs

There have been gangs in the United States for a long time, but the "crews" (gangs) of today are different. Gangs have always been a substitute family for troubled young people. But today's gangs are less about controlling territory and more about business. Gang members now have cellular phones to go with their weapons.

Vietnamese gangs are a special case. After the Vietnam War, many Vietnamese families and villages were forced to leave and split apart. Many of the "Boat People" fleeing Vietnam were robbed on boats and ended up in refugee camps. Young Vietnamese, many of them Amerasians—the children of American soldiers and Vietnamese women—arrived in the United States with few or no family ties. The older Vietnamese were so busy worrying about survival that many kids, who knew little English, were left with no supervision. They didn't feel at home anywhere. Some older Vietnamese criminals got these kids involved in crime: robbery, car theft, and so on.

These gangs are mobile. Moving from place to place, they live in motels and pick Vietnamese communities as their victims. Many Vietnamese keep their money and valuables at home, and the gangs know this. The violence in this community continues.

Answer the questions. Check *True* or *False*.

	True	False
1. Gangs haven't changed over the years.	_____	_____
2. Vietnamese gangs are made up mostly of older criminals.	_____	_____
3. Amerasians are half American, half Vietnamese.	_____	_____
4. Vietnamese gangs do not usually harm their own people.	_____	_____
5. The reason many of these kids become gang members is that they need a family and a place to call "home."	_____	_____

UNIT 10

MACHINES FOR COMMUNICATION

OVERVIEW

Objectives

Skills and Structures

Talk about people's problems	Read a bar graph
Understand recorded messages	Read about and solve problems
Understand conversations	Use an idea map to present ideas
Read instructions for voice mail	Use the conditional with *will*
Make a technology time line	Use phrasal verbs

SCANS Competencies

Participate as member of a team: Student Book, Person to Person, Page 112; Understand systems: Student Book, Reading for Real, Page 113; Acquire and evaluate information: Student Book, Culture Corner, page 114

Realia

Cassette recorder, preferably with counter

Blank audiocassette tape (one for every two students)

Photocopies and overhead projector transparency of long-distance telephone bills

Newspaper ads for beepers and/or cellular phones

Instructions for using an answering machine

Instructions for using a fax machine

Newspaper story with two-word verbs and pronouns

Videotape recording of telephone companies' long-distance ads

ACTIVITY NOTES

Page 109

Scene 1

Preparation

Ask learners the following questions and write their responses on the board:

- What are machines for communication?
- Which ones do you have at home?
- Which ones do you have at work?
- Which ones do you use regularly?
- Which ones have you never used?
- Which ones would you use in your country?

Presentation

After reading the Scene, ask students to discuss the following question in small groups: how do they feel about talking to a machine instead of a live person when they call a company?

Extension

Do a class survey to find out which long-distance telephone companies people in the class use. If learners need more practice reading or making graphs, have them work in groups and use the information from the survey to make pie graphs.

Page 110

Sound Bites

Before You Listen

Preparation

Have a class discussion about answering machines. Ask learners to raise their hands if they have an answering machine at home. Do a class survey to find out what language(s) learners use for their messages. Then ask them to share stories about problems they have had with answering-machine messages.

Presentation

Ask students to read the sentences they wrote in the Vocabulary Prompts to the class. Clarify any confusion students have.

Listening Script

1. Hi. This is Joe from Painter Pros. I wanted to start painting your house tomorrow. I'll be home after 8:00 P.M. if you need me to reschedule the job. My number is 672-0119.

2. Mr. Lopez, this is Carlos at We Fix Doors. I got your message about a broken garage door. If you'll be home tomorrow morning, I can fix it around 10:30. If this is OK with you, call me back at 1-800-994-DOOR.

3. You have reached 266-9986. We can't come to the phone right now. If you leave your name and number, we'll get back to you ASAP. Leave your message after the beep.

4. Hi. This is Lydia. I'm calling for Bertha. Listen, I got your message about picking you up at the airport on Friday. I have a meeting until 4:00, so if there is a lot of traffic, I might be late. Anyway, if you don't see me at the gate, I'll meet you at the baggage claim area. Have a safe trip. See you soon.

5. Hello. this is the Attendance Office at Heights High School. Please give your student's name, ID number, and the reason for the absence. Homework assignments are sent home only after three days of absence. If you don't call before 7:30 A.M. to request assignments, they will not be available.

6. You have reached 220-9887. I'm sorry, but I can't come to the phone now. Please leave a brief message with your name, date, and the time you called. If this is an emergency, call 660-123-4567 and ask to have me paged.

Answers to Exercise 1

1. he'll be home after 8:00 P.M.

2. be in her area around 10:30.

3. get back to you ASAP.

4. meet Bertha at the baggage claim area.

5. call the Guidance Office to request homework assignments.

6. leave a brief message with your name, date, and the time you called.

Your Turn

Extension

For additional listening practice after learners have written messages for their phones, play the tape or read the listening script again (or as many times as needed) and do one of the following activities.

Option 1: Use the messages for dictation practice.

Option 2: Ask learners specific questions about each of the messages. For example, for the first recording ask, "What is Joe's phone number?"

Option 3: Divide learners into ability groups or pairs. Assign each pair two messages to dictate to each other. (Message 3 is appropriate for lower-level learners, and Message 5 is appropriate for higher-level learners.)

Page 111

Spotlight on Conditional with *Will*

Preparation

Before learners read the examples in the Spotlight Box, check their comprehension of the concept of possible consequences. Write the words *Action* and *Possible Consequence* on the board. Have learners turn back to page 110 and read the six Sound Bites sentences aloud. Write the sentences on the board as learners read them. Ask learners to identify the action and possible consequence in each sentence.

Presentation

After learners have read the first example in the Spotlight Box, point out the difference in punctuation between the first and the second sentence.

Exercise 2

Preparation

Discuss key vocabulary words by asking the following questions:

- How many people have electric alarm clocks? What happens when the electricity goes off?
- What kinds of machines use remote controls? Do you have any machines with remote controls at home?
- What does it mean if a computer freezes? What does *reboot* mean?

Extension

Ask learners to rewrite sentences 1–6 in Exercise 2, using the format of the second example in the box. Select students to write the new sentences on the board.

Answers to Exercise 2

1. d   2. b   3. c   4. f   5. a   6. e

Page 112

Person to Person

Preparation

Ask students to read the conversations silently. Then ask one or two questions about each one. Here are some example questions:

- What does Otilia want to tape?
- What did Martin send?
- What's stuck in the toaster?
- What's in the cabinet next to the stove?

Extension

After learners have listened to the conversations, write the words *Action* and *Possible Consequence* on the board. Have volunteers read the sentences with future conditional in conversations 1–3. Write the sentences on the board under the headings above.

Ask for volunteers to re-write the three sentences on the board, using the second pattern in the Spotlight Box on page 111.

Workbook

Workbook pages 55 and 56 can be assigned after learners have completed Student Book page 112.

Page 113

Vocabulary Prompts

Presentation

Ask students to share their sentences with the class. Clarify any vocabulary students still don't understand.

Reading for Real

Preparation

Do a survey to find out how many learners have voice mail at home or work. Encourage learners to share any interesting experiences or problems they have had with voice mail with the rest of the class.

Presentation

Depending on the level of your students, you may want to present the reading point by point. These types of instructions can be confusing, even to native English-speakers.

Extension

 Option 1: For sequencing practice, copy several simple sets of instructions on sentences strips. Have learners work independently or in groups to put the instructions in order.

Option 2: Divide the class into small groups based on ability. Give each group a set of written instructions for using voice-mail, sending a fax, programming a VCR, or using a photocopy machine. Match the instructions to the groups' ability. Ask the groups to write five multiple choice or *true/false* sentences about the instructions.

Have the groups exchange instructions with another group and answer the questions. Have the first group check the second group's answers.

Answers to Exercise 3

1. a   2. b   3. b   4. a   5. c

Talk About It

Presentation

If students cannot think of any disadvantages to voice mail, give them some examples.

Page 114

Culture Corner

Presentation

To check comprehension of the time line, ask students to name the year in which the following things were invented: telegraph, radio, television, helicopter.

In Your Experience

Extension

 Option 1: Have students work with partners or in groups to make a list of technology inventions for the future. Encourage learners to be as creative as they can.

Option 2: Have students select one future invention, draw it, write an explanation, and share it with the rest of the class.

Page 115

Scene 2

Preparation

1. Tell students to turn back to page 109 and re-read it.
2. Ask learners what they think will happen in Scene 2. Write their predictions on the board.

Refer back to the predictions to see which were correct after learners have read and discussed Scene 2.

Sound Bites

Before You Listen

Preparation

Have students work in pairs to compare their phone habits in their native country with their phone habits in the United States. Have they changed their habits at all? How?

After You Listen

Extension

1. Ask learners to keep a log for three days of who they talk to on the phone at home, why, and how long they speak. Have them make a chart in class to prepare for the three days. Have learners share their logs with a partner or group. Encourage learners to analyze their phone habits. Have them categorize their phone calls if possible (friends, telemarketing, family, and so on.) Ask learners to share any interesting conclusions with the rest of the class.

2. Bring in videotaped television commercials for long-distance telephone services. Have learners make a chart to complete while they watch the commercials. The left column of the chart should have boxes for the name of each commercial. The remaining columns can be labeled *liked the most, liked the least, believed the most, believed the least,* or other categories you want learners to consider. Have learners decide which commercial they liked the most (and least), believed the most (and the least), or would make them switch to that company.

Listening Script

Luis:	What's new?
Roberto:	This is. Take a look at my latest phone bill.
Luis:	Wow! Didn't you use your phone this month?
Roberto:	Sure I did. My son did, too. He even called Mexico a few times to talk to his cousins.
Luis:	So is it a mistake?
Roberto:	No, it isn't. We figured out a few ways to lower our bill, and they worked.
Luis:	What did you do?
Roberto:	When someone calls long distance and leaves us a message, we don't call back until after 8:00 P.M.
Luis:	What else do you do?
Roberto:	Well, we look up numbers in the phone book instead of calling information. And, we changed our long-distance phone company. Long distance calls are 10 cents a minute and local calls are four cents.
Luis:	Hey, I think I'll look into doing the same things!

Answers to Sound Bites

Roberto's List

1. Call back after 8:00 P.M.

2. Look up numbers in the phone book instead of calling information.

3. Change your long distance company.

Page 116

Spotlight on Phrasal Verbs

Preparation

Encourage students to memorize the two-word verb combinations, as there are no specific rules about which prepositions go with which verbs. Native speakers learn the correct pairings of verbs and prepositions by listening and practice, not by learning rules.

Presentation

After students have read the examples in the Spotlight Box, have them turn to the Appendix. Explain that phrasal verbs are very common in English.

Exercise 5

Preparation

1. Write the phrasal verbs in Exercise 2 on the board. Divide learners into small groups. Have each group write definitions from the words on the board. Have each group read its definitions aloud to the class. Discuss and then accept or correct the groups' definitions.

2. Remind learners that two-word verbs have meaning only as a unit. Tell them that if they look up the verbs and prepositions separately in a dictionary, they will not understand the meaning of the words. Remind learners that in many dictionaries they can find the meaning of the two-word verb by looking up the verb and reading down the definitions to find a reference for the verb plus the specific preposition. Learners of English often don't realize that many dictionaries provide this special help with two- and three-word verbs.

Answers to Exercise 5

1. pick up	2. keep on
3. look up	4. call up
5. call back	6. hang up

Person to Person

Preparation

In small groups, have students quickly scan the conversations for unfamiliar words and share them with the class. If no one can provide a definition or example, explain the word. Students' unfamiliar words or phrases may include the following: *What's taking you so long?*, *I'll call you back.*, *bagel*, *unplug*, *shock*, and *flashlight*.

Spotlight on Separable Phrasal Verbs

Preparation

Again, encourage learners to memorize the separable two-word verbs on this page.

Exercise 6

Preparation

Review personal pronouns. For each sentence in the Spotlight Box, ask learners which word (noun) the pronoun refers to.

Answers to Exercise 6

1. Pick up the phone / Pick it up.
2. Call Stacey up. / Call her up.
3. Hang the phone up. / Hang it up.
4. Look the names up. / Look them up.
5. Drop the letters off. / Drop them off.
6. Turn the volume down. / Turn it down.

Your Turn

Extension

Choose a story from the newspaper that has two-word verbs and liberal use of pronouns. Duplicate the story for learners. It's a good idea to enlarge the story before you make copies for learners so it's easy for them to read and mark up. If you don't have access to a photocopier with an enlarger, type it doubled-spaced. Have learners circle the pronouns and draw arrows to the nouns they replace. Have learners underline two-word verbs. Use an overhead projector transparency to review learners' answers.

Workbook

Workbook pages 57 and 58 can be assigned after learners have completed Student Book page 117.

Activity Masters

Activity Master 10-1 can be assigned after learners have completed Student Book page 117 and Workbook page 58. This master is a concentration game for practicing two-word verbs.

Presentation

1. Duplicate Activity Master 10-1 on colored card stock, or laminate if possible. Paper is OK if you don't have access to card stock or lamination. Give one paper and a pair of scissors to each pair or group.
2. Have learners cut out the cards, shuffle them and lay them out on a table in five rows across and six rows down.
3. In turn, each person picks up three cards. If the three cards have a verb, noun, and preposition that can be used correctly to make a meaningful sentence, the person keeps the cards. (Remind learners that you are available to settle disputes about what is meaningful.) Tell learners that if the cards don't make a meaningful sentence, they should put them back in the same places.
4. When all the cards have been taken, the person with the most sets of cards wins.

Extension

Have learners write sentences with the words from their cards.

Page 118

Get Graphic

Preparation

In small groups ask students to discuss the following questions:

- What was your first experience with computers?
- How old were you?
- Was it in your native country or the United States?
- Did you enjoy it?

Exercise 7

Preparation

Write the words and their definitions on separate sentence strips and do a whole-class match-up activity. Then follow up with the group activity of writing the answers in the book.

Answers to Exercise 7

1. g   2. e   3. a   4. f   5. c   6. d   7. b

Answers to Exercise 8

1. word-processing   4. 20
2. information retrieval   5. desktop publishing
3. 90

In Your Experience

Extension

Have students make a graph analyzing class computer use by age.

Activity Masters

Activity Master 10-2 can be assigned after learners have completed Student Book page 118. This master provides learners with additional practice in reading graphs and working together in groups.

Presentation

1. Divide learners into groups. Duplicate one copy of Activity Master 10-2 for each pair or group.

   Read the directions aloud and answer any questions learners may have. Circulate while learners work on their questions to provide needed help with grammar or vocabulary.

2. After learners finish writing questions, have each pair or group exchange questions they have prepared with another group, which will write answers to those questions. Ask the original groups to check the answers. Debrief by asking having each pair or group choose one question and answer to share with the rest of the class.

Issues and Answers

Preparation

Ask students to think of technology or machines that they use at work, either in the United States of in their native country. Have they ever had problems with these machines? Have volunteers share their problems with the class. Encourage other students to suggest solutions.

Workbook

Workbook pages 59 and 60 can be assigned after learners have completed page 120.

ANSWERS FOR PROGRESS CHECKS

Progress Check A

Speak or Write

Answers will vary. Here are some possible answers:

1. He has gotten a phone bill for $1,500.00.
2. The telephone company didn't make a mistake. Roberto's son made the calls.
3. He made his son pay him back for the telephone bill, and he changed to a cheaper long distance telephone company.

Listening Script

1. This is Shirley at Dr. Jourdan's office. This message is for Liz. I'm calling to confirm your six-month checkup on Monday at 8:30. Please call back to let us know if you'll be coming.

2. Hi. This is Liz Minicz. I will not be able to make my checkup on Monday because I can't take off work. I'll call again later to reschedule my appointment. Sorry for the inconvenience.

Listen

1. False   2. True   3. False   4. False   5. True

Progress Check B

Language Structures

1. Look (it) up
2. Look (it) over
3. turn off
4. wipe off
5. Hang (your coats) up

Content

1. b   2. d   3. c   4. a   5. b, d

ANSWERS TO ACTIVITY MASTERS

Activity Master 10-1

Answers will vary.

Activity Master 10-2

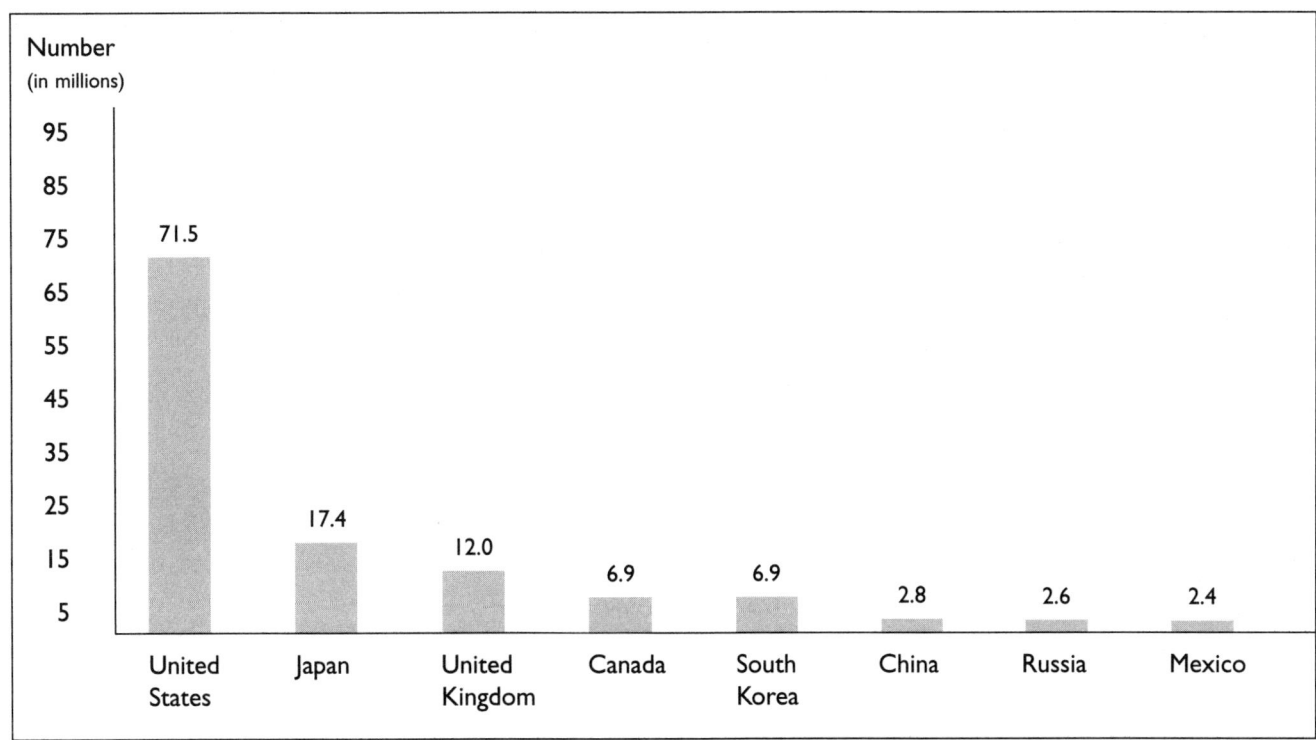

WORKBOOK ANSWERS

Practice 1

1. leave	2. will be (will get)	3. get
4. will have	5. will be (will get)	6. drive

Practice 2

Answers will vary. Here are some possible answers:

1. his pay will be docked.
2. will be more employable.
3. he finds a better one.
4. he pays less for insurance.
5. he will get a raise
6. he saves enough money
7. he'll be tired.
8. Carlos is not at work.

Practice 3

Answers will vary. Here are some possible answers:

1. If you eat dinner too late, you'll have trouble sleeping.
2. If you buy too many things on credit, you'll have to pay high interest.
3. If you shop carefully, you'll save money.
4. If you have two jobs and go to school, you'll come home exhausted.
5. If you watch TV and listen to the radio in English, you'll learn English faster.

Practice 4

1. bring out	2. plug. . . in	3. put away
4. wipe off	5. call up	

Practice 5

1. I ran into them at the supermarket.
2. Look out for him.
3. Pick them up.
4. When did you get over it?
5. How well do you get along with them?

Practice 6

1. figure out	5.	shut off
2. throw away	6.	look over
3. keep on	7.	start over
4. turn down	8.	put away

REPRODUCIBLE MASTER
UNIT 10

WORKBOOK ANSWERS

Practice 7

1. numeric

   $65.00/$8.00 monthly service fee

   Call beeper and leave a number.

   Advantage: cheap

   Disadvantage: Don't know if call is an emergency.

2. alphanumeric

   $150.00/$25.00 monthly fee

   Call operator. Operator leaves a typed message.

   Advantage: Know the message without calling the person.

   Disadvantage: Expensive

3. voice mail

   $300.00/$45.00 monthly fee

   Calls can leave a message up to four minutes long.

   Advantage: Callers can leave messages.

   Disadvantages: Expensive

REPRODUCIBLE MASTER
UNIT 10
PROGRESS CHECK A

SPEAK OR WRITE

Look at the pictures from Unit 10. Use the questions below to talk or write about each picture.

Questions

1. Why is Roberto shocked?

2. Did the telephone company make a mistake? Explain.

3. How does Roberto solve his problem?

LISTEN

While you listen, check *True* **or** *False.*

	True	False
1. Dr. Jourdan called.	_____	_____
2. Shirley wants to remind Liz about her appointment.	_____	_____
3. Liz doesn't have to call back.	_____	_____
4. Liz forgot about the appointment.	_____	_____
5. Liz will reschedule her appointment.	_____	_____

UNIT 10   PROGRESS CHECK B

LANGUAGE STRUCTURES

Use the phrasal verbs in the list below to complete the sentences.

hang up   turn off   look up   look over   wipe off

1. If you don't know a classmate's telephone number,
   _____ it _____.

2. If you finish your test early, _____ it
   _____.

3. _____ the VCR before you unplug it.

4. Before you leave class, _____ the board.

5. _____ your coats _____ on the
   hooks over there.

CONTENT

Circle the correct answer.

1. Where would you hear the following message?
   "We're busy right now. Leave your name and number, and we'll
   get back to you."
   a. VCR instructions   b. answering machine
   c. computer   d. remote control

2. Which of the following is not a machine for communication?
   a. CD player   b. computer   c. FAX   d. battery

3. What is a disadvantage of voice mail?
   a. You can record messages.   b. You can save messages
   c. You don't know if someone listened to your message.
   d. You don't know if someone recorded your message.

4. Which would be best to show all the jobs you've had and when
   you had them?
   a. time line   b. pie graph   c. bar graph   d. table

5. Two ways to lower your phone bill are to
   a. Call information when you don't know a phone number.
   b. Return calls when rates are lower.
   c. Use call waiting.
   d. Install an answering machine.

Name _____ Date _____

ACTIVITY MASTER 10-1

PHRASAL VERB CONCENTRATION GAME

Note: See Teacher's Manual page 162 for complete directions on this activity.

✂

call	your parents	back
apply	a job	for
hang	the phone	up
turn	the iron	off
look	the number	up
take	your coat	off
put	the books	away
wipe	the board	off
plug	the VCR	in
fill	the application	out

Name _____ Date _____

MORE GRAPHIC SKILLS

The number of computers in the world has grown quickly since 1985. Read the table below about the numbers of computers in 10 countries in four different years.

COUNTRIES WITH THE MOST PERSONAL COMPUTERS
(in millions)

Country	1985	1989	1992	1995
United States	19.1	44.5	64.6	91.5
Japan	1.8	5.9	10.2	17.4
United Kingdom	1.8	4.8	7.9	12.0
Canada	0.8	2.4	4.1	6.9
South Korea	0.10	0.40	1.4	6.9
China	0.09	.36	.87	2.8
Russia	0.08	0.31	0.88	2.6
Mexico	0.12	0.46	1.14	2.4

With a group, write five questions about the table above. For example, write, "Which country had the most computers in 1985?" Give the questions to another group to answer. Check the group's answers.

Now, with a partner, make a bar graph that shows the number of personal computers for each of the countries above in the year 1995.   Show your graph to another pair. Ask the pair to check your work for accuracy.

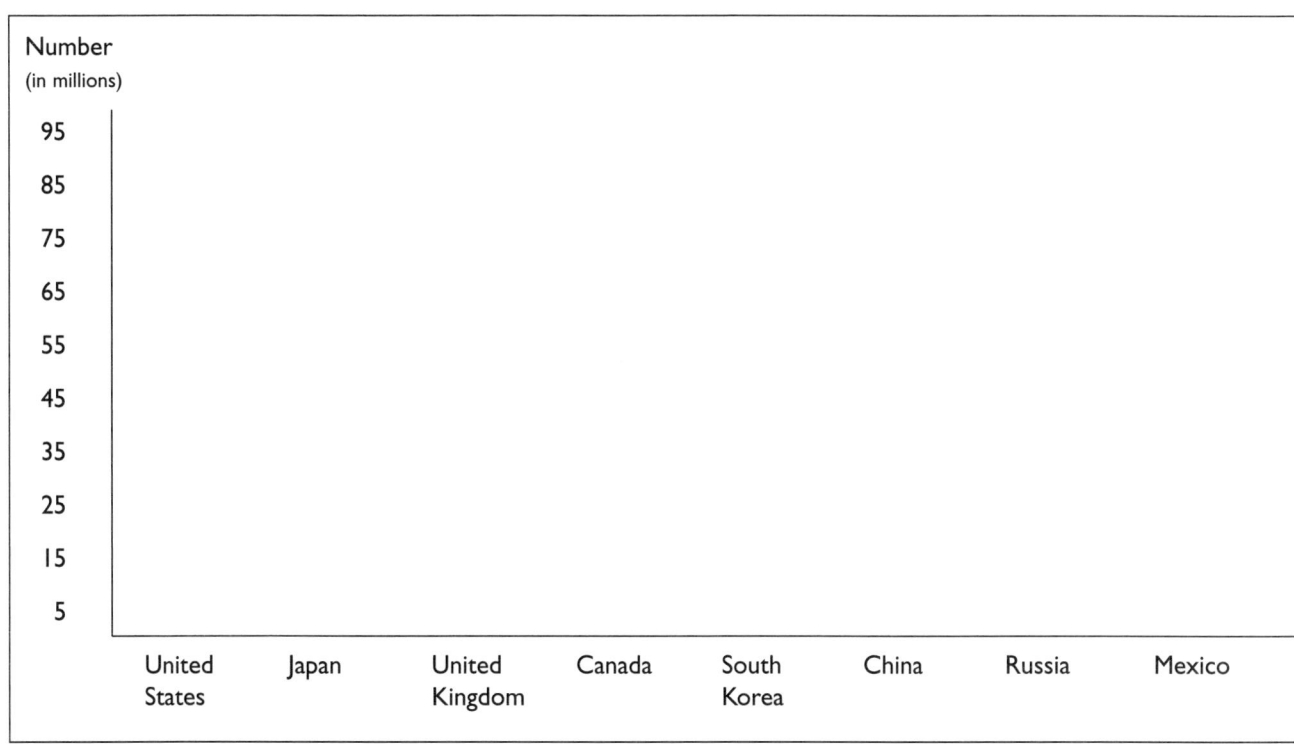